Chick Flicks 2

GROUP'S
DINNER
A AND **MOVIE**

Friendship, Faith, and Fun for Women's Groups

Group

Loveland, Colorado

www.group.com

Group resources actually work!

This Group resource incorporates our R.E.A.L. approach to ministry. It reinforces a growing friendship with Jesus, encourages long-term learning, and results in life transformation, because it's

Relational
Learner-to-learner interaction enhances learning and builds Christian friendships.

Experiential
What learners experience through discussion and action sticks with them up to 9 times longer than what they simply hear or read.

Applicable
The aim of Christian education is to equip learners to be both hearers and doers of God's Word.

Learner-based
Learners understand and retain more when the learning process takes into consideration how they learn best.

Group

Credits

Movie Mavens: Stephanie A. Carney, Linda Crawford, Amy Nappa, Kerry VanDusen, Roxanne Wieman, and Jill Wuellner
Project Manager and Head Snack-Maker: Amber Van Schooneveld
Executive Developer: Amy "I never miss the Oscars" Nappa
Chief Creative Officer: Joani "Hand me the tissues" Schultz
Art Director/Cover Art Director and *Lord of the Rings* Fanatic: Andrea Filer
Photography: Rodney Stewart
Interior Designer: Joey Vining
Copy Editor: Dena Twinem
Print Production Artist: YaYe Design
Cover Designer: Samantha "Pass the popcorn" Wranosky
Illustrator: Alan Flinn
Production Manager: DeAnne Lear
Senior Project Manager: Pam Clifford

Special thanks to Emily Branzell, Alexa Brolsma, Brianna Brolsma, Hannah Garland, Dayle Gilbert, Jordyn Greene, Madilyn Leuthauser, Moriah Leuthauser, Abbi Stratton, Heather Stratton, and Ashlyn Wong.

Library of Congress Cataloging-in-Publication Data
Group's dinner and a movie : chick flicks 2 : friendship, faith, and fun for women's groups / [contributing authors, Stephanie A. Carney ... et al.]. -- [Rev. ed.].
     p. cm.
  ISBN 978-0-7644-3709-0 (pbk. : alk. paper)
 1. Female friendship--Religious aspects--Christianity. 2. Small groups--Religious aspects--Christianity. 3. Motion pictures--Religious aspects--Christianity. 4. Film criticism. I. Carney, Stephanie A.
  BV4647.F7G76 2008
  259.082--dc22
10 9 8 7 6 5 4 3 2 1   17 16 15 14 13 12 11 10 09 08
Printed in the United States of America.

2008001711

Table of Contents

Introduction

Food, movies, talking, more food, more talking…sound like a great evening with girlfriends to you? If so, you're gonna love *Chick Flicks 2!*

So many of you enjoyed the tasty meals, wonderful spiritual discussions, and time getting to know girlfriends better with the first *Chick Flicks*, we just had to supply you with more of these gatherings for your women's ministry, small group, or youth group. You can host a chick-flick night once a quarter, once a month, or anytime your group is up for something a little different.

This book is packed with 12 movies that will get you and your girlfriends laughing (and crying) together and exploring some of the spiritual issues that affect your life. Here's how it works: You'll invite friends over, and together you'll prepare and enjoy a themed meal. Chatting with girlfriends while chopping, stirring, eating, and laughing together can help you learn more about one another while really becoming a community. It can also encourage some of the most enriching discussions you'll ever have, so we've included Mealtime TalkStarters to get you all thinking and talking about the themes in the movies you'll be watching.

Before each event, read through the ingredients list and recipes, and ask women to volunteer to bring different ingredients. Most recipes serve eight, so make sure to plan according to the size of your group. Some of the recipes are also best made ahead of time, so look for the "Make Ahead of Time" icon for these recipes. Or, if you don't want to take the time to cook, we've also included Easy Option Meals—tasty, themed meals you can pick up at the store or a local restaurant. For the complete experience, we've included decoration ideas to take your event to the next level!

The movies we've selected contain deep spiritual themes that are applicable to any woman's daily life. There's adventure, loss, romance, dreams, grace, and forgiveness. The themes can powerfully teach us about the God we serve and how to follow him better. Use the discussion questions after each movie to get your group really thinking about the themes and ways to apply the lessons to everyday life. We've also included Bible verses that will get you started in the right direction.

We pray these chick-flick events will enrich your friendships and draw you closer to God. Start the show!

Deciding Which Movies Are Best for Your Group

The movies in this book were handpicked because women love them and they can encourage some great spiritual discussions. That said, a movie's inclusion in this book doesn't mean we endorse all of the content in that film. **If you haven't seen one of the movies, screen it to determine how appropriate it is for your group *before* showing it to your entire group.** Included in each chapter are the rating of the movie and a note if there is questionable material you need to be aware of. Know the women in your group and what is appropriate for their age and faith, and know the movies before you decide to use them.

Is It Legal to Show These Movies to My Small Group?

In general, federal copyright laws do allow you to use videos or DVDs for the purpose of home viewing as long as you aren't charging admission. However, you may feel more comfortable if you purchase a license. Your church can obtain a license from Christian Video Licensing International for a small fee. Just visit www.cvli.org or call 1-888-302-6020 for more information. When using a movie that is not covered by the license, we recommend directly contacting the movie studio to seek permission to use it.

Come join us for
Chick Flicks 2

We'll watch
Pride & Prejudice
and enjoy a genteel British meal!

When: _____
Time: _____
Where: _____
_____
_____
RSVP: _____

Come join us for
Chick Flicks 2

We'll watch
A League of Their Own
and enjoy tasty ball-park treats!

When: _____
Time: _____
Where: _____
_____
_____
RSVP: _____

Come join us for
Chick Flicks 2

We'll watch
Return to Me
and enjoy a heartwarming spaghetti dinner!

When: _____
Time: _____
Where: _____
_____
_____
RSVP: _____

Come join us for
Chick Flicks 2

We'll watch
My Big Fat Greek Wedding
and enjoy a Greek feast!

When: _____
Time: _____
Where: _____
_____
_____
RSVP: _____

Cut the invitations along dashed lines.

Come join us for
Chick Flicks 2

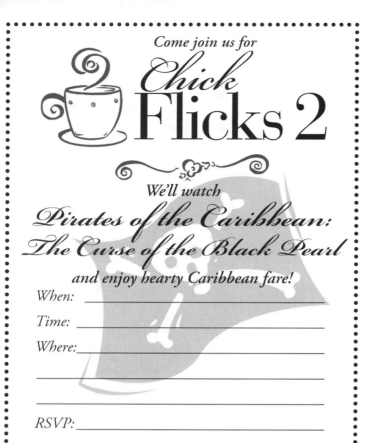

We'll watch
Pirates of the Caribbean: The Curse of the Black Pearl
and enjoy hearty Caribbean fare!

When: _____

Time: _____

Where: _____

_____

_____

RSVP: _____

Come join us for
Chick Flicks 2

We'll watch
Akeelah and the Bee
and enjoy delicious sack-lunch treats!

When: _____

Time: _____

Where: _____

_____

_____

RSVP: _____

Come join us for
Chick Flicks 2

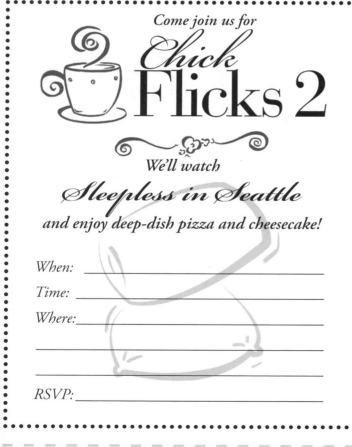

We'll watch
Sleepless in Seattle
and enjoy deep-dish pizza and cheesecake!

When: _____

Time: _____

Where: _____

_____

_____

RSVP: _____

Come join us for
Chick Flicks 2

We'll watch
To Kill a Mockingbird
and enjoy delectable Southern fare!

When: _____

Time: _____

Where: _____

_____

_____

RSVP: _____

Cut the invitations along dashed lines.

Come join us for
Chick Flicks 2

We'll watch

Moulin Rouge!

and enjoy the flavors of France!

When: _____

Time: _____

Where: _____

_____

_____

RSVP: _____

Come join us for
Chick Flicks 2

We'll watch

Freaky Friday

and enjoy Chinese food favorites!

When: _____

Time: _____

Where: _____

_____

_____

RSVP: _____

Come join us for
Chick Flicks 2

We'll watch

Cinderella

and enjoy a magical fairy-tale dinner!

When: _____

Time: _____

Where: _____

_____

_____

RSVP: _____

Come join us for
Chick Flicks 2

We'll watch

The Philadelphia Story

and eat a socialite's supper!

When: _____

Time: _____

Where: _____

_____

_____

RSVP: _____

Cut the invitations along dashed lines.

Pride & Prejudice

Genre: Drama   **Length:** 127 minutes   **Rating:** PG

QUICK PLOT: *Rumor, gossip, and secret affection. Misunderstanding, reconciliation, and love.*

Why This Movie Is Great for Chicks:
A fairytale minus the fairy godmother and mean stepsisters, this story will make every romantic swoon. But the themes go beyond romance—to pride, humility, love, and forgiveness.

DINNER
Elizabeth's Heart-ichoke Chicken
Presumptuous Pecan Salad
Prideful Soufflé

MOVIE SNACKS
Humble Pie
Coffee

SUPPLIES

If you're cooking your meal together, you may want to talk to everyone in your group and divide the ingredients list before your event. Keep in mind that some items cost more than others. Perhaps several people would like to share the cost of the more expensive items while others each bring a couple of items.

If you decide to have guests prepare the meal before the event, photocopy the recipes in this book and assign each recipe to one woman.

RECIPES

ELIZABETH'S HEART-ICHOKE CHICKEN

Elizabeth's heart goes through a lot in this movie—from being hardened in prejudice and pride, to being broken and softened by love.

- 1 teaspoon paprika
- 1 teaspoon salt
- ½ teaspoon pepper
- 8 boneless skinless chicken breasts (about 4 ounces each)
- 4 tablespoons butter, divided

- two 14-ounce cans water-packed artichoke hearts, rinsed, drained and halved
- 1 pound fresh mushrooms, sliced
- 3 cups reduced-sodium chicken broth, divided
- ¼ teaspoon dried tarragon
- 4 tablespoons all-purpose flour

Combine the paprika, salt, and pepper in a small bowl, and sprinkle over both sides of the chicken. In a large nonstick skillet, melt 2 tablespoons of butter and cook chicken until browned on both sides.

Transfer chicken to a 4-quart baking dish which has been coated with nonstick cooking spray. Top with artichokes and set aside.

In the same skillet, sauté mushrooms in remaining butter until tender. Stir in 2½ cups of broth and the tarragon, and bring to a boil. Whisk the flour and remaining ½ cup of broth together until smooth, and then stir into mushroom mixture. Bring to a boil; cook and stir for 2 minutes or until thickened.

Pour over chicken. Cover and bake at 350 degrees for 25 to 30 minutes or until chicken juices run clear. Serves 8.

Easy Option Meal

If you'd like to be like the genteel Brits in this flick and have someone else prepare your feast, stop by your local grocery store and purchase a rotisserie chicken, good crusty bread, and a bag of salad for a simple but classy dinner. For dessert, pick up an apple pie—and call it Humble Pie!

RECIPES

PRESUMPTUOUS PECAN SALAD

2 tablespoons butter

1 cup pecan halves

4 tablespoons sugar

½ cup dried cranberries

8 cups baby spinach

raspberry vinaigrette dressing

In a small skillet, melt the butter. Add pecans and cook over medium heat until nuts are toasted, about 4 minutes. Sprinkle the pecans with sugar. Cook and stir until sugar is melted. Transfer to a greased, foil-lined baking sheet. When pecans have cooled completely, break them apart.

In a large bowl, toss the spinach, cranberries, and pecans with the raspberry vinaigrette dressing. Serves 8.

PRIDEFUL SOUFFLÉ

1 stick butter, melted

1 can corn, drained

1 can creamed corn

1 cup sour cream

1 beaten egg

1 package Jiffy cornbread mix

¼ cup chopped onion

1 teaspoon garlic

salt and pepper

Mix all ingredients together and pour into a greased 9x13-inch pan. Bake at 350 degrees for 45 to 60 minutes, or until a toothpick comes out clean. Serves 8.

 Make Ahead of Time

HUMBLE PIE

2 cups all-purpose flour

1 teaspoon salt

½ cup vegetable oil

3 tablespoons milk

2 cups diced fresh or frozen rhubarb, thawed

2 cups fresh or frozen raspberries, thawed

1 cup sugar

3 tablespoons quick-cooking tapioca

Glaze:

6 tablespoons powdered sugar

2 teaspoons water

¼ teaspoon almond extract

Combine the flour and salt in a bowl. Add the oil and milk and toss with a fork until the mixture forms a ball. Shape the dough into a disk and wrap in a large piece of plastic wrap. Place in the refrigerator for at least an hour.

(continued on next page)

Helpful Hint

You can simplify this recipe by using pre-made pie-crust dough, available at the grocery store.

RECIPES

In another bowl, combine the rhubarb, raspberries, sugar, and tapioca. Let stand for 15 minutes. Unwrap the dough and place on a parchment-lined baking sheet. Cover with waxed paper and roll the dough into a 12-inch circle. Remove and discard the waxed paper.

Spoon the fruit mixture into the center of the dough, to within 2 inches of the edges. Fold the edges of dough over, covering a portion of the fruit and leaving the center uncovered. Bake at 400 degrees for 25 to 30 minutes or until the crust is golden brown and the filling is bubbly. Remove to a wire rack.

Combine the confectioners' sugar, water, and almond extract and stir until smooth. Drizzle over the pie and serve. Serves 8.

Helpful Hint

If using frozen fruit, measure the amount of fruit while it's still frozen, then thaw completely. Drain, but do not press out the liquid.
Any type of fruit can be substituted for the rhubarb and raspberries. Especially good are apples or peaches.

COOKING TOGETHER

1. When everyone has arrived, ask for a volunteer to prepare the Prideful Soufflé. (This takes 45 to 60 minutes to bake, so you may want to assemble it ahead of time, based on how much time you have planned for your night.)

2. Once the soufflé has been placed in the oven, ask two volunteers to work together to prepare Elizabeth's Heart-ichoke Chicken. Place in the oven after the soufflé has cooked about 20 to 25 minutes.

3. While the chicken and soufflé are cooking, recruit two additional volunteers to prepare the pecans and remaining salad ingredients according to the directions. Make sure to cool the pecans on a piece of greased foil or parchment paper, so they won't stick to the foil.

Helpful Hint

Be sure everyone washes her hands before the cooking begins.

Decorations

This is the perfect event for women who love the Victorian age and romance. Pull out all the beautiful items you've inherited, received as gifts, or purchased yourself and rarely get an opportunity to use. This is the time to set the table with a linen tablecloth, a table runner, china, and crystal goblets. A floral centerpiece or candelabra would be perfect for your British meal.

Place crystal or glass candelabra with taper candles around the room, and light the candles just before guests arrive.

If you have any floral arrangements or plants, use these to accent the room, along with any doilies, glass decanters, and silver you might have.

This is a fun event for women to don any formal wear they might have…an old prom or bridesmaid dress would be perfect. If anyone has a broad-brimmed hat that ties under the chin with a ribbon, it'll give her that English countryside look. You also might consider having feathers, pearls, or small flowers for women to place in their hair.

Pull out any classical music, particularly piano or violin (or the soundtrack to this movie), to complete the atmosphere.

Mealtime TalkStarters

• Tell about someone you secretly admired in the past. Did you ever let that person know about your admiration?

• Tell about a time your first impression of someone was way off base. What happened?

4. Ask anyone who isn't cooking to set the table and prepare beverages for everyone.

5. When the chicken and soufflé are done cooking, and the salad has been tossed, transfer all dishes to the table.

6. Have everyone gather around the table, and ask someone to pray.

7. When you are done, clean up the dishes and put leftovers in the refrigerator.

8. Serve your snack, Humble Pie and coffee, before the movie.

LET'S WATCH A MOVIE!

Pride & Prejudice

THE PRE-SHOW

Serve the Humble Pie and coffee and head to the area where you're showing the movie. While enjoying your snack, take this Jane Austen Classics Trivia Quiz and see how everyone does. Then it's movie time!

JANE AUSTEN CLASSICS TRIVIA QUIZ

1. Name some of the Jane Austen books that have been made into major motion pictures.

2. What movie starring Alicia Silverstone is a modern version of Emma?

3. How many times has *Pride & Prejudice* been made into a movie?

4. What movie starring Renée Zellweger is loosely based on *Pride & Prejudice?*

5. What famous actress/director has ties to the movie versions of *Sense and Sensibility, Emma,* and *Pride & Prejudice?*

 Answers

1. *Emma, Sense and Sensibility, Persuasion, Mansfield Park, Pride & Prejudice, Northanger Abbey*

2. *Clueless*

3. Twice—in 1940 and 2005. It has been made into a TV mini-series at least six times, and several other movies are loosely based on the plot.

4. *Bridget Jones's Diary*

5. Emma Thompson. She starred in and wrote the screenplay for *Sense and Sensibility,* is the older sister of Sophie Thompson, who played Miss Bates in *Emma,* and assisted in writing dialogue for *Pride & Prejudice.*

THE SHOW
Pride & Prejudice

Genre: Drama

Length: 127 minutes

Rating: PG

Plot: *Pride & Prejudice* is the story of Elizabeth Bennet (Keira Knightley), a young woman in 18th-century England from a family of five girls. With no sons to become heir to the family inheritance, Mrs. Bennet is always on the lookout for available (and rich) bachelors to wed her daughters.

One daughter, Elizabeth, meets Mr. Darcy (Matthew Macfadyen), a man of considerable wealth whom she finds immediately prideful and repellent.

Elizabeth and Mr. Darcy find themselves together in various social situations, which all strengthen Elizabeth's dislike of Mr. Darcy. When her own family comes into an embarrassing position, however, Mr. Darcy graciously and privately saves her family, and Elizabeth is forced to rethink her prejudice toward him.

THE POST-SHOW

After the movie, use some or all of these questions to discuss the spiritual themes of *Pride & Prejudice.*

What character from the movie could you most identify with? Explain.

Elizabeth bases much of her opinions of both Mr. Darcy and Mr. Wickham on hearsay, rumor, and assumption. When have you found yourself in a similar situation?

Share your thoughts about Mr. Collins and his ultimate marriage to Charlotte. Who benefited most from this marriage, and why? If you put yourself into Charlotte's shoes, what would you have done?

Mr. Darcy helps the Bennet family without their knowledge and saves them from social embarrassment. Has anyone ever helped you anonymously? If so, tell about that situation.

Is there someone in your life who might need your help? How would remaining anonymous affect you? How would it honor God?

Mrs. Bennet is overly concerned with the future of her daughters, and it affects everyone around her. How do your worries and concerns affect those around you?

How different would life have been if Mrs. Bennet could have placed her worries in Christ's hands? How could this ease the worries of your own life?

Read Philippians 4:6-7. Have you ever experienced the peace of God despite worrisome circumstances?

PRAYER

Before heading home, make sure to end the evening with a prayer together!

Bible Passages

Use these Bible passages to deepen your discussion:

- 1 Samuel 16:7—God looks at the heart.

- James 2:2-4—Don't show favoritism.

- Philippians 4:6-8—Recipe for peace in worrisome situations.

- Matthew 6:1-4—Do good deeds anonymously.

A League of Their Own

Genre: Comedy/Drama/Sports   **Length:** 128 minutes   **Rating:** PG

QUICK PLOT: *Sisters. Baseball. Perseverance. Dreams. Adversity. Camaraderie. Friendship. Spirit. Jealousy. Sacrifice. Bitterness. Redemption. Love. Legacy.*

Why This Movie Is Great for Chicks: *This story brings out the "You go girl!" from every woman. It's a history lesson heralding women who stepped out of the cultural norm during World War II and earned the respect of the country by standing together through adversity and personal struggles. With themes of unconditional love, perseverance, and unity displayed between the women, the movie gives depth to its already fun story.*

Note: *The PG rating is for language. There are also some sexual references and innuendo.*

DINNER
Peaches' Peachy Pulled Pork Sandwiches
Seventh Inning Stretch Slaw
Fresh peach slices (Go Rockford Peaches!)
Potato chips
Soda pop, iced tea, or lemonade

MOVIE SNACKS
Cracker Jacks or caramel corn (purchased from the store)
Root beer floats

SUPPLIES

If you're cooking your meal together, you may want to talk to everyone in your group and divide the ingredients list before your event. Keep in mind that some items cost more than others. Perhaps several people would like to share the cost of the more expensive items while others each bring a couple of items.

If you decide to have guests prepare the meal before the event, photocopy the recipes in this book and assign each recipe to one woman.

RECIPES

Easy Option Meal

Need a faster meal option? Go for some classic baseball food from the grocery store. Grab hot dogs and buns with a variety of condiment fixings (ketchup, relish, mustard, and even sauerkraut!). Or head to the freezer section for corn dogs, french fries, onion rings, or soft pretzels. Add old-fashioned bottled root beer or cream soda to drink. For dessert, stop at the bakery for a peach pie in honor of the Rockford Peaches.

SEVENTH INNING STRETCH SLAW

2 tablespoons sesame seeds

½ cup sliced almonds

1-2 tablespoons butter

1 bag coleslaw or shredded cabbage

4-5 scallions, sliced

1 package ramen noodles, broken into little pieces

Dressing:

½ teaspoon salt

½ teaspoon garlic powder

½ cup oil

3 teaspoons vinegar

2 teaspoons sugar

1 oriental ramen flavor packet

Brown sesame seeds and almonds in butter. Put slaw, scallions, nuts, and sesame seeds in a medium-sized bowl. In a smaller bowl, mix the dressing ingredients.

Right before serving, add ramen noodles and dressing. If you add noodles and dressing too early, it becomes soggy. Serves 8.

ROOT BEER FLOATS

8 ounces root beer per person

1-2 scoops vanilla ice cream per person

maraschino cherries and whipped cream (optional)

Put scoops of ice cream into a tall glass and slowly pour root beer over the ice cream. Keep remaining root beer handy to pour over ice cream after the foamy topping is eaten. Top with whipped cream and maraschino cherries if desired.

RECIPES

Make Ahead of Time

PEACHES' PEACHY PULLED PORK SANDWICHES

2½ pounds boneless pork loin roast

two 12-ounce cans ginger ale

1 can peach nectar (look in the juice aisle)

½ cup peach preserves

salt and pepper to taste

barbecue sauce

whole grain buns or hoagie rolls

Place roast in a slow cooker, and cover with ginger ale. Cook on low for 8-10 hours. Use two forks to take the roast out of the pot and place in a large serving bowl. Shred the pork with a fork and steak knife or with two forks.

In a separate bowl, mix peach preserves with ½ cup peach nectar. Pour over the shredded pork and mix. Increase proportions of preserves and nectar for a sweeter pork. Add salt and pepper to taste. Serve on bread of choice, and set out barbecue sauce as an additional topping. Makes 8-10 sandwiches.

Decorations

It's baseball time! Decorate with baseball pennants, posters, baseballs, bats, and mitts throughout. If you like, ask the women to come in baseball attire. Suggest T-shirts from their favorite teams, baseball caps, knee-high socks, and tennis shoes. Add an athletic skirt to sympathize with what the women had to wear while they played. Don't forget the lipstick, because according to the All-American Girls Professional Baseball League rules of conduct, lipstick must always be worn. For serving, go for simplicity with disposable plates, cups, napkins, and utensils. Old-fashioned parfait glasses are a nice touch for the root beer floats. In the background play 1940s swing music or search for "baseball music" at your local library to add the finishing touches for the theme.

COOKING TOGETHER

1. In the morning, start the pulled pork in the slow cooker. It needs to cook on low at least 8 hours (no more than 10), so plan ahead.

2. Have the first two people who arrive begin making the Seventh Inning Stretch Slaw.

3. Other volunteers can set out the buns, plates, napkins, silverware, and other serving items, and open the bags of chips.

4. Have one woman pull the pork from the pot into a large serving bowl and shred. Add peach sauce according to the recipe. Cover until ready to eat. Set a bottle of barbeque sauce next to the serving bowl for those who desire it.

5. Have another volunteer set up drinks and a bowl of ice.

6. Have another woman slice the fresh peaches.

7. When you're finished eating, clean up the dishes and put leftovers in the refrigerator.

8. Serve your floats and Cracker Jacks or caramel corn just before the movie.

Mealtime TalkStarters

- What sports have you played or been a big fan of? Were you ever on a team that had a winning season? If so, tell about that.

- The movie centers on sisters and friendships. What defines a sister? Who has been a "sister" to you?

LET'S WATCH A MOVIE!

A League of Their Own

THE PRE-SHOW

Serve the root beer floats and hand out the Cracker Jacks or caramel corn, and then head to the area where you're showing the movie. During your snack, take the Baseball Lingo Trivia Quiz and see how everyone does. Then it's movie time!

BASEBALL LINGO TRIVIA QUIZ

1. A wallop, a tater, a moonshot, a jack, and a dinger are all terms for…?
   a. a shut out
   b. a home run
   c. a strikeout

2. If your team is at bat and there are "ducks on the pond" (runners on base), who do you *not* want at bat?
   a. a "crackerjack" who hits "salami"
   b. a "masher" and a "salad"
   c. a "banjo hitter" who hits a "can of corn"

3. Which "award" is given to a player who strikes out four times in one game?
   a. Platinum Sombrero
   b. Olympic Rings
   c. Golden Sombrero

4. Which phrase is *not* lingo for a hard-hit ground ball?
   a. a "worm burner"
   b. a "lawnmower"
   c. a "daisy cutter"

5. The expression "ate him up" refers to a ball that…
   a. a fielder had trouble handling.
   b. a batter couldn't hit.
   c. a pitcher pitched, but was easily hit.

Helpful Hint!

For a fun prize for the quiz winner, award a tube of bright lipstick or sparkly lip gloss. Have several on hand in case of a tie.

Answers

1. b
2. c, You would *not* want a weak batter (banjo hitter) hitting an easily caught ball (can of corn), which would be an out for your team. You *would* want (a) a very skilled player (crackerjack) who hits a grand slam home run (salami), or (b) a home-run hitter (masher) with an easy pitch (salad).
3. c (The other two are those who strike out five times in one game.)
4. b
5. a

THE SHOW
A League of Their Own

Genre: Comedy/Drama/Sports

Length: 128 minutes

Rating: PG for some language, and there are several sexual references

Plot: During World War II, professional baseball is likely to be shut down since many of the players enlisted. Chicago club owner Walter Harvey gives his protégé Ira Lowenstein the job of figuring out how to keep baseball going. His idea is to start a women's baseball league (All-American Girls Professional Baseball League), and girls are recruited from around the country.

Sisters Dottie (Geena Davis) and Kit (Lori Petty) are working at their family's dairy when a scout recruits the talented Dottie. She declines, but the scout strikes a bargain that Kit can come if Dottie comes, too. Both are chosen to play for the Rockford Peaches, joining a diverse group of girls and playing under the management of Jimmy Dugan (Tom Hanks). Jimmy, a former professional baseball star, does not believe girls can play baseball. Neither do the spectators who come to watch. The movie follows the girls both on and off the field as they form friendships, battle through criticism and personal struggles, and create a legacy by playing the game they love.

THE POST-SHOW

After the movie, use some or all of these questions to discuss the spiritual themes in *A League of Their Own.*

Which character do you relate to most? What character qualities do you see in the movie that you admire?

Kit wants to see the world and repeatedly states her desire to do something "special." Dottie would be content to be married and raise a family. What defines something "special" in your opinion? How does our culture define it?

How do women's roles and their place in society differ from the 1940s to today? How is biblical womanhood the same or different from what is portrayed in the movie? in our culture today?

What message does the movie share about unity and friendship that you could apply to your own life?

The women in this movie had to battle criticism, stereotypes, and cultural norms. What battles do you find yourself fighting today? In what areas do you feel like you're going against the flow? Are these battles worth fighting or not?

Bible Passages

You may want to use these Bible passages during your movie discussion:

- Galatians 5:22-26—Good character comes from the Holy Spirit.

- Proverbs 27:3-6, 9-10, 17—It's worth it to stick with friendships.

- 1 Corinthians 12:12-26—Diversity is part of being in God's family.

When has a hardship in your own life allowed you to see more clearly what mattered most?

Jimmy Dugan says to Dottie, "It's supposed to be hard. If it wasn't hard, everyone would do it. The hard is what makes it great." When have you seen this statement to be true in your own life?

The movie shows the legacy left by women's baseball and how it changed the women who played. What legacy do you want to leave? What are you doing now to make this happen?

PRAYER

Before heading home, make sure to end the evening with a prayer together!

Return to Me

Genre: Romantic Comedy/Drama **Length:** 115 minutes **Rating:** PG

QUICK PLOT: *Bob's heart is broken when his wife tragically dies in a car accident. Grace's heart is dying until she gets a second chance at life through a transplant. Both soon discover that only true love can keep their hearts alive with hope for a better future.*

Why This Movie Is Great for Chicks: *Tears of sadness, tears of joy, and lots of laughs in between make this heartwarming story of love lost and found a chick favorite. The positive depictions of the influence of Christian faith and family in this movie are refreshing and encouraging.*

Note: *There is one family in this movie that uses offensive language.*

DINNER
Irish Spaghetti
Italian Garlic Bread
Tomatoes and Mozzarella
Bottled water (and straws!)

MOVIE SNACKS
Biscotti (purchased from the store)
Coffee/tea

SUPPLIES

If you're cooking your meal together, you may want to talk to everyone in your group and divide the ingredients list before your event. Keep in mind that some items cost more than others. Perhaps several people would like to share the cost of the more expensive items while others each bring a couple of items.

If you decide to have guests prepare the meal before the event, photocopy the recipes in this book and assign each recipe to one woman.

RECIPES

IRISH SPAGHETTI

1½ pounds spaghetti

2 tablespoons olive oil

1 medium onion, chopped fine

4 cloves garlic, minced

2 pounds of fresh spinach or 2 packages (10 ounces) frozen chopped spinach, thawed and drained

1½ cups skim milk

1½ cups chicken broth

¾ cup grated Parmesan cheese, plus additional cheese for topping

½ teaspoon pepper

Cook spaghetti according to package directions. While spaghetti is cooking, heat olive oil in a large saucepan over medium heat. Add onion and garlic, and cook about 5 minutes until onion is soft. Add spinach, milk, chicken broth, grated cheese, and pepper. Bring mixture to a boil, then reduce heat and simmer until slightly thickened—about 3 minutes. Use hand blender to puree sauce or pour sauce in two batches into blender to puree. Add sauce to cooked spaghetti and toss to mix. Top with freshly grated Parmesan cheese. Serves 8.

ITALIAN GARLIC BREAD

2 loaves Italian bread

olive oil

fresh garlic cloves

Preheat oven to broil. Slice bread into ½-inch-thick slices, and place on baking sheets. Place baking sheets in oven and toast bread, turning after top is lightly browned. Remove and let cool. Peel several garlic cloves and lightly rub whole cloves across one surface of each slice of bread to impart garlic flavor. Lightly drizzle olive oil over garlic bread slices or leave plain. Serves 8.

Easy Option Meal

For a quick and easy meal, order takeout spaghetti and garlic bread for eight or cook spaghetti and serve with bottled sauce and frozen prepared garlic bread. To add an Irish touch of color, pick up a green spinach or lettuce salad and bottled dressing. To tie in with the movie, be sure you serve bottled water with a straw with your meal! Find assorted flavors of Italian biscotti in the specialty cookie aisle at your supermarket to serve with coffee or tea for dessert.

RECIPES

TOMATOES AND MOZZARELLA

4 large ripe tomatoes

two 8-ounce balls fresh mozzarella

fresh basil

olive oil

red wine vinegar

Cut tomatoes and mozzarella into thin slices. Arrange tomatoes on serving platter and then arrange cheese slices on top. Top with fresh basil leaves. Serve drizzled with olive oil and vinegar. Serves 8.

Decorations

"Love your heart" is the theme of this dinner and movie event. Have your guests come dressed in everything red, and ask at your local American Heart Association for any "Go Red for Women" promotional items you could share. Decorate with red flowers, red tablecloths, and red and white dishes. Cut large and small hearts out of red paper, and scatter them around the edges of the floor of your entryway and on your table. Tie red balloons outside, and greet your guests with a big hug! You might even want to stage a "Go Red" mini fashion show before dinner so everyone can show off her beautiful red outfit. Play Frank Sinatra and Dean Martin love songs in the background to make the show complete! Consider purchasing inexpensive heart pins to give to your guests as a special remembrance of the evening.

COOKING TOGETHER

Helpful Hint

Be sure everyone washes her hands before the cooking begins.

1. Before your group arrives, arrange three preparation areas for making spaghetti, bread, and the tomato salad. Set out cutting boards, knives, measuring cups, two large pots, and baking sheets.

2. As guests arrive, assign volunteers to three teams to make the Irish Spaghetti, Italian Garlic Bread, and Tomatoes and Mozzarella according to the recipe instructions.

3. When the food is ready, ask someone to pray, and then serve dinner family-style at your red-themed table.

4. To tie in with the movie, be sure to serve bottled water with a straw during dinner!

5. When you've finished eating, clean up the dishes and put leftovers in the refrigerator.

6. Serve your biscotti with tea and coffee before the movie.

Mealtime TalkStarters

- Our meal is an unlikely blend of Irish- and Italian-themed food. How can we blend different tastes and cultures together to make healthy friendships? Why is it important for us to mix with people who are different from us?
- Share what the phrase "love your heart" means to you.

LET'S WATCH A MOVIE!

Return to Me

THE PRE-SHOW

Serve the biscotti with coffee or tea, and head to the area where you're showing the movie. During your dessert snack, take this Love Your Heart Trivia Quiz and see how everyone does. Then it's movie time!

LOVE YOUR HEART TRIVIA QUIZ

1. How many times does your heart beat in a day?

2. What are two risk factors for heart disease in women that you can't control?

3. What are two risk factors for heart disease in women that you can control?

4. According to the American Heart Association, what symptoms in addition to chest pain are women more likely than men to experience during a heart attack?

5. What color has the American Heart Association adopted for its campaign for women's health?

THE SHOW
Return to Me

Genre: Romantic Comedy/Drama

Length: 115 minutes

Rating: PG for language and thematic elements

Plot: Bob's heart is broken when his wife tragically dies in a car accident. Grace's heart is failing, and she will die unless a donor gives her a second chance at life. Bob buries himself in his work, and Grace sequesters herself in her garden—until the night Bob ventures out to eat at Grace's family's restaurant. Inexplicably, they are drawn to each other

Helpful Hint

Motivate your guests to "love their hearts" by taking the free online "Go Red Heart CheckUp" at the American Heart Association Web site for women: goredforwomen.org.

Answers

1. Roughly 100,000 times a day. That's 2.5 million beats during an average lifespan.

2. Age and heredity. As a woman ages, her risks increase; if she has a family history of heart disease, her risks increase.

3. Smoking and obesity. Others include diabetes, high blood pressure, and high cholesterol.

4. Pain in jaw or shoulder, weakness, and sweating.

5. Red. "Go Red for Women, Love Your Heart" is their motto.

and soon begin dating and dreaming of a different future. But Grace has a secret she is afraid to reveal. When she accidentally discovers her secret has a fateful connection to Bob's life, she realizes the truth could either break their hearts or bind them together forever.

THE POST-SHOW

After the movie, use some or all of these questions to discuss the spiritual themes of *Return to Me.*

Grace was given a second chance at life, yet she still struggled with unhappiness. Why? When have you experienced sadness when others expected you to be happy?

Bob was paralyzed by his wife's tragic death. When have you felt unable to "move on" in life? How did you get through that time?

This is a fictional story of two people being brought together who then discovering an amazing link. Do you have a story from your own life of an amazing connection with a friend that was discovered after the friendship was established?

Grace's grandfather prayed fervently for her through her illness and recovery. How did faith help Grace and her family get through that difficult time? How does your faith help you in difficult times?

What role did the older characters in the movie play in helping Grace and Bob's relationship? What positive role do older mentors play in your life?

Bob made the difficult choice to donate his wife's heart so someone else could live. How is this like or unlike the sacrifice God made for us through Jesus Christ?

When Grace discovered the truth about her heart, she said "What was God thinking?" As a Christian, do you sometimes question God? How does God help us discover his plans and purposes in our lives?

Read this statement from the American Heart Association:

"By loving your own heart, you can save it. When women learn to love their hearts, they can appreciate their health, their life, and their loved ones." Discuss what loving your heart means to you.

You may want to use these Bible passages during your movie discussion:

- Matthew 22:37—Love the Lord.

- John 10:10—Abundant life in Jesus.

- Hebrews 11:1—Definition of faith.

- Proverbs 3:5-6—Trust in God.

Jesus commanded us in Matthew 22:37 to "love the Lord your God with all your heart." Share what that Scripture means to you.

PRAYER

Before heading home, end the evening with a prayer together. Have each woman place her hand over her heart and pray together to ask for God's help to continue to love their hearts, love the Lord, and love each other!

My Big Fat Greek Wedding

Genre: Romantic Comedy   **Length:** 95 minutes   **Rating:** PG

QUICK PLOT: *All Toula's father wants is for her to marry a nice Greek boy. But Toula soon realizes she wants more than just tradition in her life.*

Why This Movie Is Great for Chicks: *What woman can resist a great makeover story? In addition to being an uplifting tale of transformation, this movie tackles honoring your parents, persevering in developing your talents, dealing with cultural differences, and discovering God's perfect plan for your life.*

Note: *This movie contains one episode of the Lord's name used in vain, some crude language, and sexuality references.*

DINNER
Traditional Greek Salad
Not-So-Traditional Greek-American Burgers
My Big Fat Bundt Cake
Mint Iced Tea

MOVIE SNACKS
Almonds (purchase almonds with a variety of seasonings on them at the grocery store)

SUPPLIES

If you're cooking your meal together, you may want to talk to everyone in your group and divide the ingredients list before your event. Keep in mind that some items cost more than others. Perhaps several people would like to share the cost of the more expensive items while others each bring a couple of items.

If you decide to have guests prepare the meal before the event, photocopy the recipes in this book and assign each recipe to one woman.

RECIPES

Easy Option Meal

For a quick and easy meal of Greek food, just stop in at your local supermarket! Pick up prepared Greek salad in the deli, pita bread, and pre-made hamburger patties. Buy a Bundt cake from the bakery for dessert and some almonds for snacks. Season the hamburgers with Greek seasoning; grill; and serve with sour cream, sliced cucumbers, tomatoes, and onions on pita bread.

TRADITIONAL GREEK SALAD

6 tomatoes

1 cucumber

1 red onion

1 green bell pepper

1 head of romaine lettuce

2 teaspoons dried oregano

8 to 12 ounces of feta cheese

15 to 20 kalamata or other Greek olives

Dressing:

½ cup olive oil

2 tablespoons red wine vinegar

1 teaspoon salt

pepper to taste

Wash vegetables and lettuce and pat dry. Cut tomatoes into wedges and green pepper into small chunks, and place in a large salad bowl. Peel cucumber, and then cut into thin slices. Cut onion in half and then into thin slices. Add both to the bowl. Sprinkle vegetables with oregano and mix well with salad tongs.

Tear lettuce into bite-size pieces and arrange on serving platter.

Blend ingredients for dressing in a small bowl with a fork, and pour over the veggies that are in the bowl. Mix well, and place these veggies on top of the lettuce on the serving tray. Top with crumbled feta cheese and olives. Serves 8.

NOT-SO-TRADITIONAL GREEK-AMERICAN BURGERS

1 pound ground beef

1 pound ground lamb

½ medium onion, grated or finely chopped

4 cloves garlic, pressed

2 slices bread, toasted and crumbled

4 teaspoons all purpose Greek seasoning

8 pita rounds

tomato and onion slices

Cucumber Sauce (recipe on page 31)

Preheat grill to medium-high heat and lightly oil. In a large bowl, combine lamb and beef with garlic, onion, bread crumbs, and seasoning, and mix well. Shape into thin oval patties, and cook on grill 5-7 minutes until cooked through. Slice cooked patties into strips.

RECIPES

Cut pitas in half to form 16 pita pockets. Spread about 2 tablespoons of Cucumber Sauce in each pita, add tomato and onion slices then meat strips. Top meat with additional Cucumber Sauce, and serve. Serves 8 (allowing two pita pockets for each guest).

CUCUMBER SAUCE:

1 large cucumber, peeled

1½ cups sour cream

2 tablespoons minced fresh mint

2 teaspoons rice wine vinegar

2 cloves garlic, minced

salt and pepper to taste

Grate peeled cucumber and squeeze dry with clean towel or paper towels. Mix cucumber with rest of ingredients in a bowl. Refrigerate until ready to serve. Serves 8.

MINT ICED TEA

1 gallon brewed or instant iced tea

fresh mint leaves

Place ice cubes in tall glass and add two or three fresh mint leaves. Pour tea over ice and serve. Serves 8.

 Make Ahead of Time

MY BIG FAT BUNDT CAKE

1 boxed lemon cake mix

one 3.4-ounce package instant lemon pudding mix

⅔ cup vegetable oil

4 eggs

1 cup lemon-lime soda

Icing:

1 cup confectioners' sugar

lemon juice

Preheat oven to 350 degrees. Grease and flour a 10-inch Bundt pan. Combine cake mix, pudding mix, and oil in a large bowl. Beat in eggs, one at a time, then slowly add lemon-lime soda. Pour batter into Bundt pan, and bake for 40-50 minutes until toothpick inserted in center comes out clean. Cool completely on wire rack, then invert on serving plate. Mix confectioners' sugar with enough lemon juice to make thin icing, and drizzle over top of cooled cake. Serves 8-10.

Decorations

Welcome your guests to the Greek islands! For decorating inspiration check out books on Greek culture at your local library. Gather or borrow plastic or ceramic pedestals, columns, and urns. Place these items in your entryway, and decorate them with silk or real plants, ivy, and tropical flowers. Drape rich colorful silky fabrics in swags for a dramatic backdrop. Ask your friends to come dressed in light summer dresses and sandals. Play soft acoustic guitar music in the background, and serve dinner on a cool white tablecloth with white plates. Decorate your table with silk grape leaf ivy. At the end of the evening, cut grape ivy into 12-inch sections, and form small ivy crowns your guests can take home as a souvenir of their "trip"!

COOKING TOGETHER

Helpful Hint

Be sure everyone washes her hands before the cooking begins.

1. Before your group arrives, arrange preparation areas for making salad and burgers. Set out cutting boards, peelers, knives, measuring cups, and two large bowls for mixing. Prepare tea and keep chilled.

2. When guests arrive, serve mint tea and have your guests form two groups for cooking. Assign one group to prepare and cook burgers and the other group to prepare the salad according to the recipe directions.

3. While burgers are cooking, have two people set up the serving area with plates and refill drinks.

4. Just before serving, set out Greek salad and arrange Cucumber Sauce, meat slices, pita pockets, and tomato and onion slices for assembly of Greek-American burgers. Have someone pray, and then serve food buffet style. Instruct guests in assembly instructions for burgers according to the recipe directions, and enjoy!

5. For dessert, serve slices of My Big Fat Bundt Cake before or after the movie.

6. When you've finished eating, clean up the dishes and put leftovers in the refrigerator.

7. Serve assorted almonds for snacking during the movie.

Mealtime TalkStarters

• What are a few of your favorite family traditions? What makes them so meaningful?

• What new traditions have you started recently? What traditions have you heard of that you'd like to start in your family?

LET'S WATCH A MOVIE!

My Big Fat Greek Wedding

THE PRE-SHOW

Serve the assorted almonds and head to the area where you're showing the movie. Take this Glimpse of Greece Trivia Quiz and see how everyone does. Then it's movie time!

GLIMPSE OF GREECE TRIVIA QUIZ

1. According to ancient Greek mythology, who is the god of love?

2. What three seas border the Greek islands?

3. What famous ancient historical site can be found in Athens, Greece?

4. What's the highest mountain in Greece?

5. What's the predominant religion of Greece?

Answers

1. Eros

2. The Aegean, Mediterranean, and Ionian seas.

3. The Acropolis, a flat-top hill strewn with ancient temples and monuments.

4. Mount Olympus, considered in ancient times to be the home of the Greek gods.

5. Greek Orthodox. The Orthodox Church considers itself the authentic continuation of the first Christian communities established by the apostles of Jesus.

THE SHOW
My Big Fat Greek Wedding

Genre: Romantic Comedy

Length: 95 minutes

Rating: PG

Plot: Toula is 30, Greek, and unmarried. All her father wants is for her to get married to a nice Greek boy. But Toula is tired of her dull life working in the family-owned restaurant—until the day Ian, a high-school English teacher, stops in. Suddenly she starts dreaming of a better and different life from what her parents expect. She undertakes a self-makeover plan and heads back to college with a new wardrobe and a fresh outlook. Toula and Ian soon meet again, and when they start dating, the cultural conflicts really start to boil over. In order for their relationship to work, Toula's father must learn to accept Ian, Ian must learn to accept Toula's family, and Toula must learn to accept herself—and her Big Fat Greek family and heritage, too!

THE POST-SHOW

After the movie, use some or all of these questions to discuss the spiritual themes of *My Big Fat Greek Wedding.*

You may want to use these Bible passages during your movie discussion:

- Ephesians 6:1-4—Responsibilities of parents and children.

- 1 Peter 3:8—Live in harmony.

- Matthew 10:29-31—Our value to God.

How strongly do you think children are influenced by their parents' expectations of them? Is American family culture as strongly influential as the Greek family culture portrayed in the movie? Why or why not?

Toula and Ian's marriage forced them to face multiple moral, cultural, and religious conflicts between their families. What was most important to Toula's family? to Ian's family? What do you think is most important to your family?

Ian told Toula his life was boring before he met her. What was it lacking that he found in his relationship with Toula? How have friends made your own life richer?

Toula initially wanted to run away and elope with Ian. Why? Would you have felt the same way as Toula? Why or why not?

The Bible tells us to honor our father and mother so that we will live a long life (Ephesians 6:2). Do you think Toula and Ian honored their parents? Explain your answer.

How important is it to maintain family traditions and values? What are some of the values and traditions your family believes are most important to preserve?

Several characters in the movie were willing to make sacrifices in order to preserve their relationships. What have you given up to preserve an important relationship? What kinds of things do we need to be willing to give up in order to preserve our relationship with Jesus?

What do you think gave Toula the courage and the hope to change her life? What area of your life is God working his makeover plan on? How do you find the courage and hope to change?

PRAYER

Before heading home, make your ivy crowns and end the evening with a prayer. Pray for God's makeover plan in your lives, and thank God for your families and your Christian heritage and traditions!

Pirates of the Caribbean: The Curse of the Black Pearl

Genre: Action/Adventure/Comedy   **Length:** 143 minutes   **Rating:** PG-13

Quick Plot: *Pirates, sword fights, cursed treasure, and true love all mix together in this action- and laugh-packed movie.*

Why This Movie Is Great for Chicks: *This movie breaks the stereotype that all women are content to be beautiful and quiet. Women need and enjoy adventure! Elizabeth Swann is sheltered and protected—yet is obsessed with the pirate's life. Elizabeth is a strong woman who's unafraid of going after the adventure for which she longs; however, the treasure she seeks comes with a price.*

Note: *This movie is rated PG-13 for violence, some frightening scenes involving skeletons and swordplay, and alcohol use.*

DINNER
Pirate's Plunder
Treasure Island Fruit Salad
Captain Jack's Crusty Bread with Paradise Spread
Barbossa's Apple Pie (purchased from the bakery)
Rum Flavored Iced Tea

MOVIE SNACKS
Treasure Chest Delights

ᴑ SUPPLIES ᴎ

If you're cooking your meal together, you may want to talk to everyone in your group and divide the ingredients list before your event. Keep in mind that some items cost more than others. Perhaps several people would like to share the cost of the more expensive items while others each bring a couple of items.

If you decide to have guests prepare the meal before the event, photocopy the recipes in this book and assign each recipe to one woman.

RECIPES

Easy Option Meal

Visit your grocery deli for a rotisserie chicken, and serve that with bottled jerk sauce. Add fresh or canned pineapple, bakery rolls, and a big bowl of brightly colored candy for dessert.

PIRATE'S PLUNDER

4 skinless, boneless chicken breasts

2 tablespoons oil

½ pound large cooked shrimp

one 16-ounce package mushrooms

2 bell peppers

1 small onion

1 cup chicken broth

1 cup Caribbean jerk sauce or marinade (find bottled marinades near the ketchup at the grocery store)

8 cups instant rice

Cut the chicken into bite-sized chunks. Place chicken and oil in a skillet and cook until chicken is done. Set aside. Chop the mushrooms, peppers, and onion, then mix these with the chicken broth and cook in a skillet until the vegetables are tender. Do not drain. Add the cooked chicken and the cooked shrimp to the skillet and add the marinade. Simmer for 15 minutes. You can add more marinade if needed. While this is simmering, cook the rice according to package directions. Spoon the plunder over the rice. Serves 8.

Helpful Hint

If you can't find jerk marinade, use one with mango or pineapple flavoring instead.

TREASURE ISLAND FRUIT SALAD

2 cans pineapple chunks, drained

2 grapefruits

2 oranges

½ cup shredded coconut

1 cup miniature marshmallows

Peel and section the grapefruits and oranges, and cut these into smaller chunks. Toss these with the other ingredients. Serves 8.

RECIPES

CAPTAIN'S CRUSTY BREAD

Pick up your favorite loaf of bread at the bakery. We recommend baguettes or a crusty loaf of sourdough. Warm bread in the oven, and slice just before serving with the Paradise Spread.

Make Ahead of Time

PARADISE SPREAD

one 8-ounce package cream cheese, room temperature

3 tablespoons honey

½ tablespoon grated lemon zest

1 cup various edible flower petals such as roses, carnations, lilacs, pansies, or tulips (find these in your yard or at the florist)

Wash the flower petals before using them. Be sure you use flowers that have not been sprayed with chemicals.

In a medium bowl, stir together the cream cheese, honey, and lemon zest. Gently fold in the petals. Transfer to a serving dish. Cover and refrigerate for at least 2 hours before serving to blend the flavors. Spread on slices of bread. Serves 8.

RUM FLAVORED ICED TEA

Add rum-flavored extract to iced tea to taste.

BARBOSSA'S APPLE PIE

Pick up an apple pie at the bakery or from the frozen section at your grocery store. Warm it before serving and, for an extra treat, top it with whipped cream or vanilla ice cream.

TREASURE CHEST DELIGHTS

Purchase candies that look like treasures, such as gold-foil-wrapped chocolate coins, tropical-flavored candies, candy necklaces, and so on. For added fun, serve these in a box that you've decorated to look like a treasure chest!

Decorations

A treasure chest filled with gold-foil-wrapped chocolate coins, tropical-flavored candies, and candy necklaces, along with plastic beaded necklaces and other toy jewelry would be a stunning centerpiece for your dinner table. Scatter some of the treats about the table, and have a few of the jewels draping over the sides of the chest.

Any island-theme décor would be appropriate and fun. Check your local party store for palm trees, parrots, and other island decorations. Provide a pirate eye patch for each guest, and encourage women to use their best pirate accents while wearing them.

Helpful Hint

Be sure everyone washes her hands before the cooking begins.

Mealtime TalkStarters

- What's the biggest adventure you've ever had?

- What's an adventure you dream of having? What can you do to make that adventure happen?

COOKING TOGETHER

1. Prepare the Paradise Spread ahead of time. Make sure you have knives and cutting mats ready for cutting up the other ingredients, a skillet for the Pirate's Plunder, and a pan large enough for the rice placed on the stove ready to go.

2. As the first guests arrive, have them begin the Pirate's Plunder, as this takes the most time to prepare. As a few more guests arrive, have them begin on the Treasure Island Fruit Salad, and have final guests work on the finishing touches, such as making the rice, setting the table, warming and cutting the bread, pouring beverages, and so on.

3. When the meal is ready, gather everyone for a brief prayer, and then enjoy your meal together.

4. When you've finished eating, clean up the dishes and put leftovers in the refrigerator.

5. Serve the apple pie either before the movie or after. Be sure to have the Treasure Chest Delights available for nibbling during the movie.

LET'S WATCH A MOVIE!

Pirates of the Caribbean: The Curse of the Black Pearl

THE PRE-SHOW

Serve the Treasure Chest Delights, and head to the area where you're showing the movie. Be sure to refill everybody's glass with the rum-flavored iced tea. During your snack, take this Johnny Depp Movie Quote Quiz and see how everyone does. Then it's movie time!

JOHNNY DEPP MOVIE QUOTE QUIZ

Each quote listed below is from one of Johnny Depp's movies. See who can identify either the character he played or the movie the quote is from. Extra points to those who know both!

1. "The waterfall is most important. Mixes the chocolate. Churns it up, makes it light and frothy. By the way, no other factory in the world mixes its chocolate by waterfall, my dear children, and you can take that to the bank."

2. "I've got a...dwarf, and I'm not afraid to use him!"

3. "I thought you'd never guess. My favorite—hot chocolate."

4. "Who amongst you is ready to tie your hopes and dreams to the sea?"

5. "Villainy wears many masks, none of which so dangerous as virtue."

Answers

1. Willy Wonka in *Charlie and the Chocolate Factory*
2. Victor Van Dort in *Corpse Bride*
3. Roux in *Chocolat*
4. J.M. Barrie in *Finding Neverland*
5. Ichabod Crane in *Sleepy Hollow*

THE SHOW
Pirates of the Caribbean:
The Curse of the Black Pearl

Genre: Action/Adventure/Comedy

Length: 143 minutes

Rating: PG-13 for action-adventure violence

Plot: This swashbuckling tale follows pirate Captain Jack Sparrow (Johnny Depp) and blacksmith Will Turner (Orlando Bloom) as they journey the south seas to rescue the love of Will's life, Elizabeth Swann (Keira Knightley). Captain Jack has his own agenda: He longs to recapture his ship, the Black Pearl, and find a forbidden treasure.

Elizabeth has been obsessed with the pirate's life from childhood. She gets more than she bargained for when she's kidnapped by the fearsome Captain Barbossa (Geoffrey Rush) and forced to prove her own savvy pirate style. Unfortunately, Captain Barbossa and his crew are under a curse. Unless a blood sacrifice is made, they are doomed forever to neither live nor die.

This movie contains adventure violence such as swordplay, some frightening scenes involving skeletons, and the use of alcohol.

THE POST-SHOW

After the movie, use some or all of these questions to discuss the spiritual themes of *Pirates of the Caribbean: The Curse of the Black Pearl.*

You may want to use these Bible passages during your movie discussion:

- Galatians 3:13-14—Christ redeemed us from the curse.

- Ezekiel 7:19—Silver and gold cannot satisfy.

- Hebrews 12:1-4—Keep your eyes on Jesus.

- Ruth 1:16-19—A woman beginning a true adventure.

Which character in the movie are you most like? Explain.

Are you content with "normal" life, or do you long for adventure and excitement as Elizabeth did? What about your life seems non-adventurous? What could you do to bring more adventure to your life?

What stereotypes did you see challenged in this movie? How can believing in stereotypes lead to problems?

Piracy literally means taking what is not yours, wanting what you do not have, taking control and getting things through your own means. By this definition, do you think you're a pirate? Why or why not?

Each of the main characters in the movie longs for something different, whether it's love, freedom, or power. What's something you once wanted and set out to get, only to discover that this did not bring the satisfaction that you sought? Explain.

Jack's compass revealed his struggle with going after what he wanted or going after what he needed. How can fixing our eyes on Jesus set us in the right direction? How can the Bible serve as a compass for our lives?

In the end, Elizabeth got more pirate adventure than she'd bargained for. What price did she pay for her adventure, and what rewards did she gain? Do you think adventure always comes at a cost? Why or why not?

Captain Barbossa and his crew suffered from a curse that doomed them to neither live nor die. How is their curse like or unlike our condition without Jesus?

The pirates in the movie have hordes of treasure, but, because of their cursed condition, they can't even enjoy an apple. Galatians 3:13 tells us that Christ freed us from the curse of sin. What do we enjoy because of that?

The Bible tells us of many women, such as Ruth, Esther, Deborah, Rahab, and Jael, who had amazing adventures. Who do you think was the most adventurous woman of the Bible, and why? Which Bible woman would you most like to be like, and why?

PRAYER

Before heading home, make sure to end the evening with a prayer together. For added fun, give each guest an apple as a reminder of the fulfillment we can have when we have a personal friendship with Jesus.

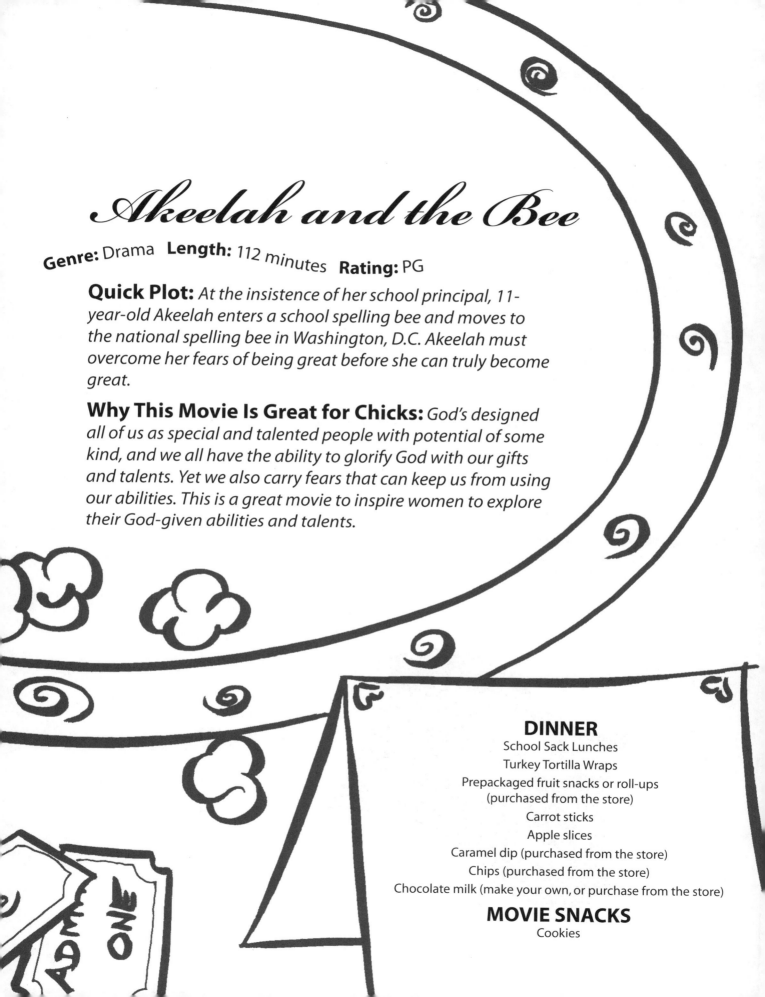

Akeelah and the Bee

Genre: Drama **Length:** 112 minutes **Rating:** PG

Quick Plot: *At the insistence of her school principal, 11-year-old Akeelah enters a school spelling bee and moves to the national spelling bee in Washington, D.C. Akeelah must overcome her fears of being great before she can truly become great.*

Why This Movie Is Great for Chicks: *God's designed all of us as special and talented people with potential of some kind, and we all have the ability to glorify God with our gifts and talents. Yet we also carry fears that can keep us from using our abilities. This is a great movie to inspire women to explore their God-given abilities and talents.*

DINNER
School Sack Lunches
Turkey Tortilla Wraps
Prepackaged fruit snacks or roll-ups
(purchased from the store)
Carrot sticks
Apple slices
Caramel dip (purchased from the store)
Chips (purchased from the store)
Chocolate milk (make your own, or purchase from the store)

MOVIE SNACKS
Cookies

❧ SUPPLIES ❧

If you're cooking your meal together, you may want to talk to everyone in your group and divide the ingredients list before your event. Keep in mind that some items cost more than others. Perhaps several people would like to share the cost of the more expensive items while others each bring a couple of items.

If you decide to have guests prepare the meal before the event, photocopy the recipes in this book and assign each recipe to one woman.

RECIPES

TURKEY TORTILLA WRAPS

8 large flour tortillas, plain or flavored

one 8-ounce container cream cheese

one 8-ounce container grated Parmesan cheese

1 pound sliced deli turkey

1 red onion, sliced thin and separated into rings

one 6-ounce bag baby spinach leaves

1 pound sliced provolone cheese (or any favorite cheese)

3 tomatoes, sliced thin

salt and pepper to taste

Spread 2 tablespoons of cream cheese on one tortilla. Sprinkle 2 tablespoons Parmesan cheese over the cream cheese. Top with turkey, some red onion, a few baby spinach leaves, 2 slices cheese, and 2-3 tomato slices, layered in order listed beginning at one edge of tortilla and spread out to cover the tortilla ⅔ of the way in. Leave an area about 2 inches wide with nothing on it. (This will make it easier to roll because the ingredients will push outward as you roll.) Sprinkle lightly with salt and pepper.

Start at the side of the tortilla with filling and begin rolling tightly toward the empty side. Hold ingredients in place as you roll tightly. Carefully place rolled tortilla on aluminum foil and wrap securely. Cut the wrapped tortilla in half. Set aside. Continue in the same manner with the other seven tortillas. Serves 8.

Helpful Hint

If you're ambitious and love to bake, then homemade cookies would be great. Any variety will do. However, it's ever so easy to pick up cookies at the store or local bakery.

Easy Option Meal

This meal is easy and time-effective as it is, but to make it even easier, substitute basic turkey sandwiches for the Turkey Tortilla Wraps. Or you could decide to have your guests bring their own sack supper. Explain to them ahead of time to bring items that truly represent a healthy school "sack" lunch. And then…just like grade school…let the lunch trading begin!

Decorations

Create signs with spelling words and their definitions on each one. Use a dictionary to find fun words that might describe the type of evening you want to have with your guests. For another fun twist, add the correct pronunciation like you might find after each word in the dictionary. Try using the same idea with your guests' names for place cards. Add color by printing out colorful bumblebees and placing them wherever a little flair is needed, such as on the corners of the signs or place cards. Check your local party store or craft store for more bumblebee decorations and ideas.

Helpful Hint

Be sure everyone washes her hands before the cooking begins.

Mealtime TalkStarters

- What were your favorite subjects in school?

- What subjects did you dread the most, and how did you get through them?

COOKING TOGETHER

1. Right before your guests arrive, lay out eight tortillas in a row on a counter or table large enough to create an assembly line.

2. Explain how the wraps are assembled, and then create the wraps in true assembly-line fashion. One person can spread the cream cheese, one can sprinkle the Parmesan cheese and apply the deli turkey, and so on. Other guests can slice apples, cut up carrots or prepare any other elements of the meal.

3. Create another assembly line to fill eight brown lunch-size bags with the wraps and other lunch munchies.

4. Don't forget to say a prayer, then enjoy your meal together.

5. Serve your cookies just before the movie starts—milk might be a great addition to that treat!

LET'S WATCH A MOVIE!

Akeelah and the Bee

THE PRE-SHOW

Serve cookies, and head to the area where you're showing the movie. During your snack have this spelling bee and see how everyone does. Then it's movie time!

SPELLING BEE

Correctly say each word, give the definition, and then use it in a sentence. The definition and a sample sentence for each word is provided. Guests should take turns trying to spell the words aloud, just like a real spelling bee. You can find more wacky and difficult words in a dictionary if you want!

1. fanciful [**fan**-si-fuh l]—imaginative; not real. *Her fanciful mind created beautiful stories.*

2. eminent [**em**-uh-nuh nt]—high, lofty. *She was an eminent member of the community.*

3. ratatouille [rat-uh-**too**-ee]—a vegetable stew of Provence, typically consisting of eggplant, zucchini, onions, green peppers, tomatoes, and garlic, served hot or cold. *Ratatouille was her main dish for supper.*

4. xanthosis [zan-**tho**-sis]—an abnormal yellow discoloration of the skin. *She was unhappy when xanthosis appeared on her skin.*

5. pulchritude [**puhl**-kri-tood]—great physical beauty and appeal. *Her pulchritude was known among women everywhere.*

Helpful Hint

The winner of the spelling bee should get a ribbon, medal, or trophy of some kind. Maybe you have an old one you could modify, or check out the party stores for inexpensive awards.

THE SHOW
Akeelah and the Bee

Genre: Drama

Length: 112 Minutes

Rating: PG for mild language.

Plot: Eleven-year-old Akeelah Anderson (Keke Palmer) has had a difficult life. Her father died when she was 6, and she misses him greatly. Her mom (Angela Bassett) works hard to provide for their family and has little time for her. Her siblings' lives are problematic at best. Though she's smart, especially when it comes to spelling words, her home environment attributes little to inspire her.

Due to all of her school absences, Akeelah is threatened with detention. At the insistence of her school principal, she enters a school spelling bee. He hopes that his school will be represented in the regional spelling bee for the first time. Much to her surprise and embarrassment, she wins. Her principal arranges coaching from an old friend, an English professor named Dr. Larabee (Laurence Fishburne), for the more prestigious regional bee. As the hope of making it to the Scripps National Spelling Bee becomes a reality, Akeelah must overcome her insecurities and problems at home, as well as with other, more advanced, spellers.

You may want to use these Bible passages during your movie discussion:

- Philippians 1:6—God will complete the good work he started in you.

- Ephesians 3:20—God can do more than we could ask or imagine.

- 2 Timothy 1:7—A fearful and timid spirit is not from God.

THE POST-SHOW

After the movie, use some or all of these questions to discuss the spiritual themes of *Akeelah and the Bee*.

Have you ever, like Akeelah, been required to become involved in something of a positive nature only to find that it brings out many fears and doubts about yourself? Explain.

Mrs. Anderson had to quickly decide how to handle Akeelah's deception about the regional spelling bee. How would you have handled this situation or a similar one?

What have you dreamed of accomplishing in your life…but have not taken action to make come true? Could you still achieve this dream? What would it take?

Dr. Larabee inspired Akeelah to achievement. Who has been an inspiration in your own life? What are you doing to pass that along to someone else?

Akeelah is asked to read a quote by Marianne Williamson. Part of that quote says, "Who am I to be brilliant, gorgeous, talented, famous? Actually who are you not to be?...We were born to make manifest the glory of God that is within us." What's your reaction to this quote? If you had to pick one of those four words to describe yourself, which one would it be and why?

Why are some people afraid to be great or do something great? Do you think you're someone who strives to be great or who hides from this goal?

Akeelah describes L-O-V-E as "that feeling where everything feels right...where you don't have to worry about tomorrow or yesterday, where you feel safe and know you're doing the best you can." How do you describe love? How does God fit into that definition?

PRAYER

Before heading home, make sure to end the evening with a prayer together.

Sleepless in Seattle

Genre: Romantic Comedy   **Length:** 105 minutes   **Rating:** PG

QUICK PLOT: *Sam is despairing in Seattle, and Annie is disillusioned in Baltimore—can love really heal his broken heart and give her hope for a better future? Through a series of quirky circumstances, they just might discover that love really can conquer all!*

Why This Movie Is Great for Chicks: *A truly great chick flick invokes both roiling laughter and gushing tears—and this one is a classic! Throw on your pj's, grab some tissues and popcorn, and enjoy!*

Note: *This movie contains themes that condone premarital sex and a few scenes with offensive language.*

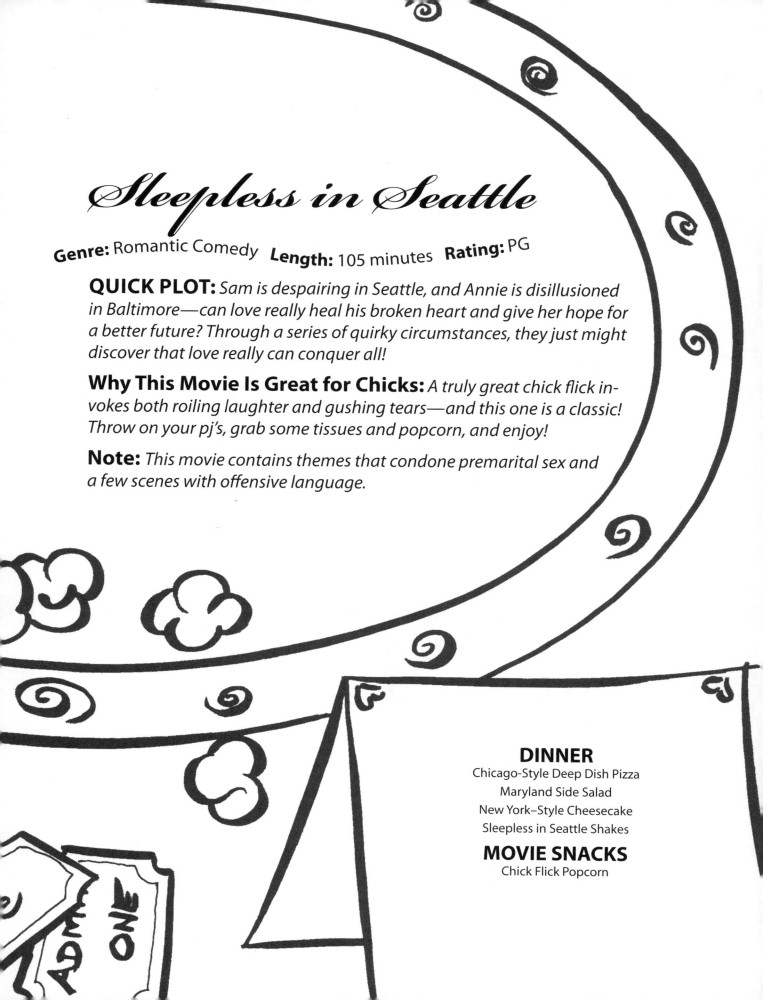

DINNER
Chicago-Style Deep Dish Pizza
Maryland Side Salad
New York–Style Cheesecake
Sleepless in Seattle Shakes

MOVIE SNACKS
Chick Flick Popcorn

SUPPLIES

If you're cooking your meal together, you may want to talk to everyone in your group and divide the ingredients list before your event. Keep in mind that some items cost more than others. Perhaps several people would like to share the cost of the more expensive items while others each bring a couple of items.

If you decide to have guests prepare the meal before the event, photocopy the recipes in this book and assign each recipe to one woman.

RECIPES

CHICAGO-STYLE DEEP DISH PIZZA

1 pound loaf frozen bread dough, thawed

1 pound sweet Italian sausage

3 cups shredded mozzarella cheese

1 small onion, chopped

two 14½-ounce cans diced tomatoes, drained

1 teaspoon dried oregano

¾ teaspoon salt

¼ teaspoon garlic powder

⅔ cup freshly grated Parmesan cheese

Preheat oven to 475 degrees. Grease an 11x15-inch pan or two round deep-dish pizza pans. Press thawed bread dough into bottom and 2 inches up the sides of pan(s).

Cook crumbled sausage in frying pan over medium-high heat until browned. Drain off fat, and spread sausage evenly over dough. Sprinkle sausage with mozzarella cheese.

To make pizza sauce, add chopped onion to frying pan and cook until onion is tender. Stir in the tomatoes, oregano, salt, and garlic powder, and cook for an additional minute to blend. Spoon sauce over cheese and top with freshly grated Parmesan.

Bake at 475 degrees on top rack in oven for 10 minutes, then reduce heat to 350 and bake for an additional 10-15 minutes until crust is golden brown. Cut into 16 pieces, and eat with a knife and fork. Serves 8.

MARYLAND SIDE SALAD

1 large bag pre-washed baby spinach

¼ cup sesame seeds

one 15-ounce can mandarin oranges, drained

one 16-ounce bottle poppy seed dressing

Put spinach, sesame seeds, and mandarin oranges in a large salad bowl. Pour on ½ bottle poppy seed dressing, and gently mix ingredients together. Add more dressing as needed to coat spinach. Serve as a side salad. Serves 8.

Easy Option Meal

What could be more fun and easy for a great chick-flick event than pizza and dessert? To make this meal even easier, order a deep-dish pizza or two. Pick up a prepared salad mix, dressing, and a New York–style cheesecake from the deli of your local supermarket. And don't forget to grab a bag of prepared popcorn to munch during the movie.

RECIPES

SLEEPLESS IN SEATTLE SHAKES

2 cups strong decaf coffee

2 cups milk

1⅓ cups sweetened condensed milk

4 tablespoons chocolate syrup

40-48 ice cubes

Make beverages two at a time in a blender as follows: Pour ½ cup coffee, ½ cup milk, ⅓ cup sweetened condensed milk, and 1 tablespoon chocolate syrup into blender. Add 10-12 ice cubes and blend on high until smooth and slightly frothy. Pour into tall glasses, and serve with a straw. Repeat 4 times to make 8 servings.

CHICK FLICK POPCORN

16 cups popped microwave or ready-made popcorn

Shake-on toppings:

Powdered cheese topping

Dry ranch dressing topping

Kettle korn topping: ¼ cup sugar, ½ teaspoon cinnamon

Place popcorn in large bowl. Scoop individual popcorn portions into large plastic cups, and allow guests to top with favorite topping. Serves 8.

 Make Ahead of Time

NEW YORK–STYLE CHEESECAKE

2½ pounds cream cheese, softened

1¾ cup sugar

3 tablespoons flour

5 eggs

2 egg yolks

¼ cup heavy cream

2 cups graham cracker crumbs

⅓ cup sugar

½ cup butter, melted

Preheat oven to 475 degrees. Lightly coat a 10-inch springform pan or 9x13-inch pan with spray oil. Mix graham cracker crumbs, sugar, and melted butter in bowl. Press cracker crust into pan and up sides slightly. Keep crust refrigerated until ready to fill.

To make filling, blend softened cream cheese, sugar, flour, eggs, and egg yolks in large mixing bowl. Add cream and mix just to blend.

Pour filling over crust, and bake for 10 minutes at 475 degrees. Reduce temperature to 200 degrees and continue to bake for one hour. Turn oven off, but leave cheesecake in cooling oven for one hour. **Note:** Cheesecake may still crack in the middle. Chill cheesecake overnight before serving. Serve plain or with your favorite fruit topping. Serves 8.

Decorations

Invite your friends to enjoy this movie at a Chick Flicks pj Party! Tell your guests to let their hair down, get in some comfy pajamas and slippers, and come over to enjoy a relaxed and fun evening watching this favorite romantic comedy. Decorate with lots of pillows, blankets, and cushions, and eat on TV trays or on the floor in the same room where you will watch the movie. You could even throw a few air mattresses on the floor for extra seating! Add extra romantic girly touches by scattering heart-themed objects around the room or using heart-themed paper plates and napkins. For added ambience, string some mini lights in the room and play soft romantic ballads for background music. Be sure to have tissues handy, and remove breakables before the pillow fight breaks out!

COOKING TOGETHER

1. Before your guests arrive, be sure to have frozen bread dough thawed according to the package instructions.

2. Arrange work area to prepare pizza with cutting board, knives, measuring cups, frying pan, and spoons. Arrange a second work area for making the salad with a salad bowl and measuring cup.

3. As guests arrive, designate one person to prepare Sleepless in Seattle Shakes in the blender, and assign others to prepare Chicago-Style Deep Dish Pizza and Maryland Side Salad according to the recipe directions.

4. Have guests enjoy shakes while making the pizza!

5. Just before serving baked pizza, have someone pray over the food and then dig in! Serve pizza with bottled water or soda, and use paper plates and napkins for easy cleanup.

6. When you've finished eating, clean up the dishes and put leftovers in the refrigerator.

7. Serve your New York–Style Cheesecake for dessert.

8. Prepare popcorn and toppings, and set out to enjoy during the movie.

Helpful Hint

Be sure everyone washes her hands before the cooking begins.

Mealtime TalkStarters

- What do you think it takes for two people to fall in love? to stay in love?

- Do you believe in love at first sight? Why or why not?

LET'S WATCH A MOVIE!

Sleepless in Seattle

THE PRE-SHOW

Pop your Chick Flick Popcorn, and set out with shake-on toppings to enjoy during the movie. Take this Sleepless Trivia Quiz and see how everyone does. Then it's movie time!

SLEEPLESS TRIVIA QUIZ

1. What's the record for the longest period without sleep?
   - 7 days
   - 11 days
   - 21 days

2. Approximately how many hours of sleep do new parents lose in a baby's first year?
   - 100-200 hours
   - 300-400 hours
   - 900-1200 hours

3. What has the greatest disruptive effect on the sleep cycle?
   - light
   - odor
   - noise

4. What percentage of the average person's life is spent sleeping?
   - one-quarter
   - one-third
   - one-half

5. What is the recommended amount of sleep for people of these ages:
   - infant
   - teenager
   - adult

 Answers

1. 11 days (264 hours). The last official record is from the 1965 *Guinness Book of World Records*. Guinness stopped supporting sleep-deprivation records due to the associated health risks.

2. Approximately 350 hours of sleep for parents is lost in the first year.

3. Noise. Especially unfamiliar noise and noise during the first and last two hours of sleep.

4. one-third

5. infant: 18 hours a day, teenager: 8 to 9.5 hours a day, adult: 7 to 8 hours a day

THE SHOW
Sleepless in Seattle

Genre: Romantic Comedy

Length: 105 minutes

Rating: PG

Plot: Sam Baldwin (Tom Hanks) has a broken heart and hasn't been interested in dating since his wife died two years ago. But his 8-year-old son, Jonah, thinks his father needs a new wife, so, in desperation, Jonah calls a nationwide radio show on Christmas Eve for help. Sam's story is heard by thousands of women, including Annie (Meg Ryan) in Baltimore, who has just become engaged to Walter. Annie suddenly becomes disillusioned with the prospect of a life with Walter and can't stop daydreaming about Sam. One day she decides she can't rest until she meets Sam in Seattle, but her plans go awry and she heads home determined to forget him and marry Walter. Then a strange letter from Seattle arrives agreeing to meet her at the top of the Empire State Building on Valentine's Day—just like the characters in the classic movie *An Affair to Remember.* Which opportunity for love will she choose?

THE POST-SHOW

After the movie, use some or all of these questions to discuss the spiritual themes of *Sleepless in Seattle.*

? What do you think the main message of this movie is?

? How was grief paralyzing Sam's life? Have you ever felt this kind of grief? If so, tell how you got past these feelings, or how you are dealing with them now.

? Sam's well-meaning friends gave him a variety of advice to help him in his grieving process. As a Christian, what do you think would be the best advice or support you could offer someone in Sam's situation?

? Why do you think Annie became engaged to Walter? What did her choice reveal about what she believed about love?

? Annie's beliefs about love changed as she sought answers from others. How are our beliefs about love challenged by seeking answers from God? What does God's Word say love really is?

? Sam and Annie never would have met if Jonah and Annie's friend Becky hadn't intervened to help. How have your friends helped you to find the right path in life? How has Jesus been a part of guiding your path?

Bible Passages

You may want to use these Bible passages during your movie discussion:

- Jeremiah 31:13—God's promise for joy.

- Psalm 42:11—God is our source of hope.

- Proverbs 3:5-6—Trusting God for guidance in our lives.

Annie and Sam were hoping for "magic" when they met. If you are single, what would you expect to feel when first meeting a future husband? If you're married, how did you feel when you first met your husband? Can our feelings always be trusted? Why or why not?

Do you believe love conquers all? Why or why not?

PRAYER

Before heading home, make sure to end the evening with a prayer together! Thank God for healing broken hearts and dreams and giving us joy and hope in the midst of any circumstance! End your night with some of that joy and laughter by starting that pillow fight you've been dying to have all night!

To Kill a Mockingbird

Genre: Drama **Length:** 129 minutes **Rating:** Not Rated

QUICK PLOT: *In the Depression-era South, lawyer Atticus Finch defends a black man against an undeserved rape charge as his kids learn about prejudice.*

Why This Movie Is Great for Chicks: *Unlike in the 1930s, women today have many opportunities to make a difference in society by showing the love and mercy of God.*

Note: *This movie contains adult themes of prejudice, rape, violence, and murder, though not graphically.*

DINNER
Boo Radley Biscuits With Jam
Southern Ham With Maple Syrup
Calpurnia's Collard Greens
Maycomb County Mashed Potatoes With Country Gravy
Iced Tea

MOVIE SNACKS
Pecan Pie (purchased from a bakery)

Easy Option Meal

If you're just too busy spreading justice around your neighborhood and workplace to cook, no problem. Order a bucket of chicken with mashed potatoes and gravy, coleslaw, and biscuits on the side. Pick up a pecan pie from the bakery, and you've got a Southern feast!

Decorations

Invite your guests to wear overalls or old blue jeans and old shirts. Kick off your shoes at the door, and spend the evening barefoot. Or, if you're cooking together, you might have your guests wear aprons like Calpurnia.

Throw some quilts over the sofa and chairs. Or pick up on the spookiness of the "boogeyman" theme by creating a "lights-out" atmosphere: no porch lights and only a few candles lit inside the house.

SUPPLIES

If you're cooking your meal together, you may want to talk to everyone in your group and divide the ingredients list before your event. Keep in mind that some items cost more than others. Perhaps several people would like to share the cost of the more expensive items while others each bring a couple of items.

If you decide to have guests prepare the meal before the event, photocopy the recipes in this book and assign each recipe to one woman.

RECIPES

BOO RADLEY BISCUITS WITH JAM

Buy a can of country-style biscuits (found in the refrigerator section of your grocery store) and a jar of your favorite jam. Bake the biscuits according to package directions.

SOUTHERN HAM WITH MAPLE SYRUP

4 pounds sliced breakfast ham steaks (find in the refrigerated meat section at the store)

½ cup maple syrup

Follow the cooking directions on the ham packaging, or grill each slice in a skillet until heated through. Drizzle with maple syrup before serving. Serves 8.

MAYCOMB COUNTY MASHED POTATOES WITH COUNTRY GRAVY

Use instant mashed potatoes and a mix for country gravy. Follow the directions on the package to make 8 servings. (Of course, if you're a purist, you can certainly peel, chop, boil, and mash *real* potatoes!)

Make Ahead of Time

CALPURNIA'S COLLARD GREENS

1 bunch collard greens (about 1½ pounds), rinsed, trimmed, and chopped (you can also use mustard greens or turnip greens)

8 slices of bacon, chopped into small pieces

2 cans chicken broth

2¾ cups water

1 tablespoon vinegar

salt and pepper to taste

Place the greens and bacon pieces in a 5-quart or larger kettle. Stir in the chicken broth, water, and vinegar. Season with the salt and pepper. Bring to a boil, reduce the heat to low, and simmer for one hour. The liquid should cook out but, if necessary, drain before serving. Serves 8.

COOKING TOGETHER

1. Start the greens an hour before your scheduled dinner time. Have someone transfer the greens to a serving dish right before you're ready to eat.

2. As guests arrive, divide the cooking responsibilities. Have one person begin warming the ham while another begins the mashed potatoes and gravy. Have another guest get the biscuits into the oven shortly before your meal is to be served. Others can set the table, serve the iced tea, and get the rest of the meal onto the table.

3. Gather for the meal, starting with a prayer of thanks, and then dig in!

4. When you've finished eating, clean up the dishes and put leftovers in the refrigerator.

5. Serve the pecan pie just before the movie begins. Now's also a great time to offer coffee if you have it.

Helpful Hint

Be sure everyone washes her hands before the cooking begins.

Mealtime TalkStarters

• What are some opportunities that women have today that they didn't have in the 1930s?

• Just about everyone had a fear of the boogeyman when they were small. What was your mental image of the boogeyman?

LET'S WATCH A MOVIE!

To Kill a Mockingbird

THE PRE-SHOW

Serve the pecan pie. During your treat, take this Civil Rights Trivia Quiz and see how everyone does. Then it's movie time!

CIVIL RIGHTS TRIVIA QUIZ

1. His actions as a president resulted in the abolition of slavery.

2. Her civil disobedience of refusing to obey a bus driver's order to give up her seat started the Montgomery Bus Boycott, one of the largest movements against racial segregation.

3. The influential and well-known "I Have a Dream" speech was given by this civil rights leader and Baptist minister.

4. This American civil rights leader played a pivotal role in the 19th-century women's rights movement to gain women's suffrage in the United States.

5. On June 11, 1963, this civil rights opponent stood in front of Foster Auditorium at the University of Alabama in an attempt to stop desegregation of that institution.

THE SHOW
To Kill a Mockingbird

Genre: Drama

Length: 129 minutes

Rating: Not Rated

Plot: Jean Louise "Scout" Finch (Mary Badham) and Jeremy Atticus "Jem" Finch (Phillip Alford) come of age when they learn of the destructiveness of racism and that their father, Atticus Finch (Gregory Peck), is capable of a lot more than they realize. Mixed into the story is a mysterious house down the street and the more mysterious Boo Radley (Robert Duvall) who lives inside.

Helpful Hint

The Hershey bar, specifically the Krackel bar (introduced in 1938) was very popular during the Great Depression. It was a luxury that cost a whole nickel. It would have been a true prize to anyone living in this era. Surprise the winner(s) of the trivia quiz with a Hershey bar.

Answers

1. Abraham Lincoln
2. Rosa Parks
3. Martin Luther King Jr.
4. Susan B. Anthony
5. Governor George C. Wallace

When Atticus is asked to defend a black man who is unjustly charged with raping a white woman, a courtroom battle ensues. The all-white jury will be difficult to sway, and despite a passionate speech by Atticus, the climate of the times is made evident by the sad ending to this movie.

THE POST-SHOW

After the movie, use some or all of these questions to discuss the spiritual themes of *To Kill a Mockingbird.*

The children in the movie were afraid of the Radley house and its occupants, but, like children, their fears were highly exaggerated. What was a fear you had as a child about something or someone you didn't understand? What do you still fear today?

Jem, Scout, and Dill severely misjudged "Boo" Radley. Describe a time you misjudged or wrongly judged another person.

Jem had a cigar box filled with treasures. What do you treasure from your childhood? If you could have one of your treasures returned to you today, what would it be?

Describe a "coming of age" moment in your life—when the innocence of your eyes and mind were diminished.

Have you experienced prejudice? If so, tell about that. Or, are you willing to admit being prejudiced against a group of people? What do you think you should do about these feelings?

Atticus Finch said to Scout: "You never really understand a person until you consider things from his point of view. Until you climb inside of his skin and walk around in it." How does this quote relate to your faith in Jesus?

What did Atticus see in his client Tom Robinson that others refused to see?

Boo Radley emerges as an unlikely hero in the movie. Who would you consider to be an unlikely hero in your life?

After seeing this movie, how are you motivated to make a difference in your world? Where would you like to begin?

PRAYER

Before heading home, make sure to end the evening with a prayer together.

You may want to use these Bible passages during your movie discussion:

- Micah 6:8—What God requires of us.

- James 2:1-4—Do not show favoritism.

- Psalm 69:32—The poor will see and be glad.

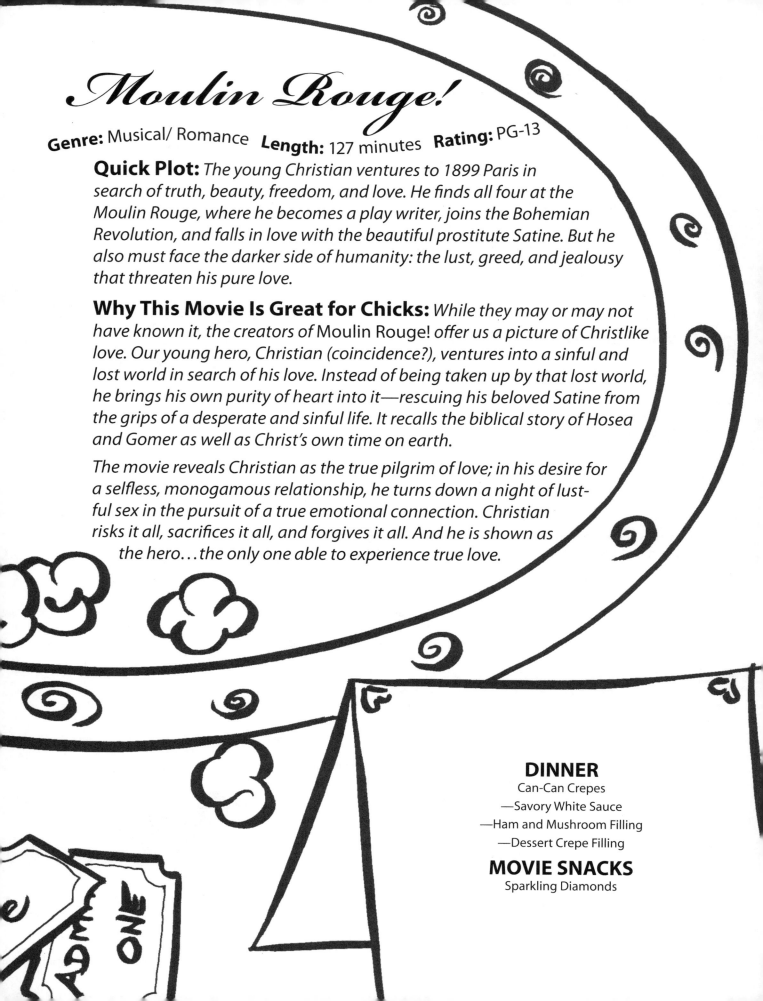

Moulin Rouge!

Genre: Musical/ Romance **Length:** 127 minutes **Rating:** PG-13

Quick Plot: *The young Christian ventures to 1899 Paris in search of truth, beauty, freedom, and love. He finds all four at the Moulin Rouge, where he becomes a play writer, joins the Bohemian Revolution, and falls in love with the beautiful prostitute Satine. But he also must face the darker side of humanity: the lust, greed, and jealousy that threaten his pure love.*

Why This Movie Is Great for Chicks: *While they may or may not have known it, the creators of* Moulin Rouge! *offer us a picture of Christlike love. Our young hero, Christian (coincidence?), ventures into a sinful and lost world in search of his love. Instead of being taken up by that lost world, he brings his own purity of heart into it—rescuing his beloved Satine from the grips of a desperate and sinful life. It recalls the biblical story of Hosea and Gomer as well as Christ's own time on earth.*

The movie reveals Christian as the true pilgrim of love; in his desire for a selfless, monogamous relationship, he turns down a night of lustful sex in the pursuit of a true emotional connection. Christian risks it all, sacrifices it all, and forgives it all. And he is shown as the hero…the only one able to experience true love.

DINNER
Can-Can Crepes
—Savory White Sauce
—Ham and Mushroom Filling
—Dessert Crepe Filling

MOVIE SNACKS
Sparkling Diamonds

ADMIT ONE

SUPPLIES

If you're cooking your meal together, you may want to talk to everyone in your group and divide the ingredients list before your event. Keep in mind that some items cost more than others. Perhaps several people would like to share the cost of the more expensive items while others each bring a couple of items.

If you decide to have guests prepare the meal before the event, photocopy the recipes in this book and assign each recipe to one woman.

RECIPES

CAN-CAN CREPES

1 cup all-purpose flour	1¾ cups milk
1 teaspoon salt	4 tablespoons melted butter
6 eggs, beaten	

To make the crepe batter, combine flour and salt in a bowl. Create a hole in the center of these ingredients, and add eggs and milk to the hole. Whisk together. Add melted butter and stir. Cover and set aside until ready to use during the get-together (if longer than a half hour, refrigerate until a half hour before use, then set out).

When you're ready to cook, heat an 8-inch nonstick skillet over medium heat. Brush the bottom with some melted butter. Carefully spoon a thin layer of the crepe batter (about 3 tablespoons) into the skillet, making sure the bottom of the pan is evenly covered. Cook until the top of the batter appears dry (about 45 seconds), then loosen it with a spatula and turn it over. Heat the other side until brown spots appear (about 30 more seconds). Repeat with the remaining batter, brushing the skillet with butter between each crepe. Stack the finished crepes on a plate. Serves 8 (three crepes each).

SAVORY WHITE SAUCE:

2 tablespoons butter	nutmeg, to taste
2 tablespoons all-purpose flour	¼ teaspoon cayenne pepper
1½ cups whole milk	¼ to ⅓ cup heavy cream
salt and pepper, to taste	

Cook butter and flour in a saucepan over low to medium heat for 2 minutes. Whisk in milk, then add seasonings. Simmer for about 15 minutes (stirring occasionally), before stirring in the cream. After stirring in cream, leave the sauce on low heat until it thickens. Serve immediately, or leave on very low heat, stirring occasionally to avoid congealing. Serves 8.

Easy Option Meal

To capture the flavors of France—without the labors—stop at a local bakery or pastry shop and pick up some ham-and-cheese croissants and a few dessert pastries such as a fruit tart, a chocolate-filled croissant, or an éclair.

RECIPES

HAM AND MUSHROOM FILLING

½ pound of button mushrooms, sliced

butter to sauté in

8 thin slices of smoked ham, diced

1 teaspoon of chopped fresh parsley

salt and pepper to taste

1½ cups grated Parmesan cheese

Sauté mushrooms in butter until soft. Add ham and parsley to mushrooms. Continue sautéing. Stir in salt and pepper. Have each woman grab one or two crepes, spoon white sauce on each crepe, add some of the mushroom and ham filling, fold it up, and top it off with a sprinkle of grated Parmesan cheese. Enjoy! Serves 8 (2 savory crepes each).

DESSERT CREPE FILLING

1 jar of Nutella spread

8 bananas

cocoa powder

Have each woman take a crepe, spread on some Nutella, slice a banana onto the Nutella, sprinkle on some cocoa powder, and fold the crepe up. Heat it for about a minute under low broiler heat—watch carefully so it doesn't burn. Take it out, sprinkle some powdered sugar on top, then eat it up. Mmmmm…Serves 8 (1 dessert crepe each).

SPARKLING DIAMONDS

4 bags of unbuttered microwave popcorn

2 sticks of butter

4 cups of sugar

Pop the popcorn and put into bowls. Melt the butter and stir it onto popcorn. While the butter is still wet, stir in sugar until all the popcorn is coated. The sugar will add a sparkle effect to the popcorn. To add a more colorful sparkle, use colored sugar sprinkles (found in the baking aisle of your grocery store).

Decorations

This movie is all about color and drama. Drape several vibrantly colored fabrics (blue, purple, red, green) on your tables, chairs, and sofas. Put out costume jewelry, feather boas, and red lipstick for your guests. Use candles and lighting to spotlight certain areas.

Print out pictures of famous locations in Paris such as the Eiffel Tower or the Moulin Rouge, and hang them in your area.

You can also emphasize the theater theme by playing music that features a live orchestra. And, for an extra flourish, tie red velvet curtains on either side of your television.

COOKING TOGETHER

1. Make the crepe batter ahead of time, and then invite the first two guests to begin cooking the crepes and stacking them for later use.

2. As more guests arrive, have one or two begin on the mushroom-and-ham filling while another gets the white sauce prepared.

3. Another guest can make the Sparkling Diamonds popcorn recipe and set that aside to enjoy during the movie.

4. Have guests prepare their own savory crepes as described in the recipe. Pray before eating. When you've finished eating the savory crepes, invite each woman to make a dessert crepe.

5. When you've finished dessert, clean up the dishes and put leftovers in the refrigerator.

6. Serve your Sparkling Diamonds snack as you settle in to enjoy the movie.

Helpful Hint

Be sure everyone washes her hands before the cooking begins.

Mealtime TalkStarters

- It's been said that women can let their emotions run away with them; when has that statement been true of you?

- Describe how you fell in love…or, if you haven't yet, describe the ideal romance.

LET'S WATCH A MOVIE!

Moulin Rouge!

THE PRE-SHOW

Serve the Sparkling Diamonds, and head to the area where you're showing the movie. During your snack, take this La Bohéme Trivia Quiz and see how everyone does. Then it's movie time!

LA BOHÉME TRIVIA QUIZ

1. When and where did the Bohemian Revolution first begin?

2. Though it doesn't exist anymore, there actually was a country named Bohemia. Where was it located?

3. What novel first popularized the ideas of the Bohemian Revolution in English?

4. What fashion in the early 21st century is based on Bohemian style?

5. What popular American musical is based on a Bohemian opera and embodies the Bohemian culture of 1980s New York City?

 Answers

1. France, in the mid-1800s, during a time when artists and creators were concentrated in lower-rent, lower-class gypsy areas of the cities. The Bohemian Revolution described the lifestyles of these marginalized artists, writers, musicians, and actors whose ideas were generally nontraditional, unorthodox, and anti-establishment.

2. Bohemia was located in central Europe, occupying the western two-thirds of the traditional Czech lands, currently the Czech Republic. The Bohemian Revolution was so called because its values were associated with gypsy culture—outsiders apart from society and convention—and it was thought those gypsies originated from Bohemia.

3. *Vanity Fair* by William Makepeace Thackeray

4. Boho-chic. This fashion is known for its countercultural influences: long "gypsy" skirts, embroidered tunics, sheepskin boots, and loose blouses. Ironically, however, the Bohemian Revolution itself was purposefully without style, considering fashion as a sort of limiting, social convention.

5. *Rent* (based on Giacomo Puccini's opera *La bohéme*)

 Helpful Hint

This movie starts out wild…the colors, movement, and noise can be startling. But don't be dissuaded, the pace settles down after the first 20 or so minutes.

While you watch those first 20 minutes, look for the subtleties: the words, winks, and color choices. There's a lot of symbolism throughout the movie, but especially at the beginning.

Throughout the movie, the filming and directing is skillfully done to portray emotion. The beginning is meant to be TOO MUCH: It's loud, vibrant, and slightly scary. The viewer—and Christian—are intended to be exhausted when it's over. Later in the movie, when the emotions change, so does the filming. Keep an eye out for how the pacing and colors mirror the emotional experience of the characters throughout the movie.

THE SHOW
Moulin Rouge!

Genre: Musical/Romance

Length: 127 minutes

Rating: PG-13 for sexual content

Plot: This is a love story. It's the love story of the young and idealistic Christian with the hardened but hopeful courtesan Satine. Set against the backdrop of the Moulin Rouge at the end of the 18th century, during the Bohemian Revolution, this movie is a feast for the senses: the color, pacing, filming, and pop song remixes take the viewer through a frenzy of emotions and end, finally, with the quietly sung anthem of the film: *The greatest thing you'll ever know is just to love and be loved in return.*

THE POST-SHOW

After the movie, use some or all of these questions to discuss the spiritual themes of *Moulin Rouge!*

Do you think it's a coincidence that the hero of the movie is named "Christian"? Why or why not? How might he symbolize a Christian in this movie? How might he symbolize Christ himself?

Do you think the film condones Satine's prostitution? Why or why not?

Throughout the movie we are given glimpses of Satine's private suffering. She is a courtesan, but she desperately desires to escape that life. And, like many caught in sin, she does the wrong things for the right reasons. When have you felt trapped by a situation or sin? How did you get out? What helped Satine out of that life?

Christian sings that "love lifts us up where we belong." How does his love lift Satine up where she belongs? How has Christ's love lifted you up where you belong?

Do you think the Moulin Rouge changed Christian, or do you think he changed the Moulin Rouge? Explain. How does Christian stand out in the indulgent world of lust that is the Moulin Rouge? How is his love for Satine different from the "love" she has experienced in the past? Describe a time you were able to make a positive impact in a negative environment.

The film says that Zidler got more than he bargained for in The Duke. Sometimes it seems like we can bargain and trick the devil…and get away with sin. Zidler certainly thought so as he signed away everything he owned and loved for a desperate dream. But how does this movie ultimately show that there are consequences—for Zidler? for Satine?

Bible Passages

You may want to use these Bible passages during your movie discussion:

- Hosea 1:2–3:5 and Hosea 14—God's love for Israel is symbolized in the marriage between Hosea and a prostitute.

- John 1:1-18—Jesus left heaven to walk among us.

- 1 John 4:7-21—Our love should be a result of Christ's love for us.

Satine loves Christian, but she also desperately wants her own dreams, to become an actress. Even once she has a new life with Christian, she still has trouble letting go of her old life. How do you think that's also true for Christians once they choose to follow Jesus? How has that been true in your life?

Zidler sings, "Does anybody know what we are living for?" What are you living for? How does Christ's love give us a reason to live? How can you communicate that reason to others who may feel lost and purposeless?

Ultimately this movie says that "the greatest thing you'll ever know is just to love and be loved in return." Do you think that statement accurately sums up this movie? Is that true for your own life? Why or why not? How might this phrase be especially true for Christians?

PRAYER

Before heading home, make sure to end the evening with a prayer together!

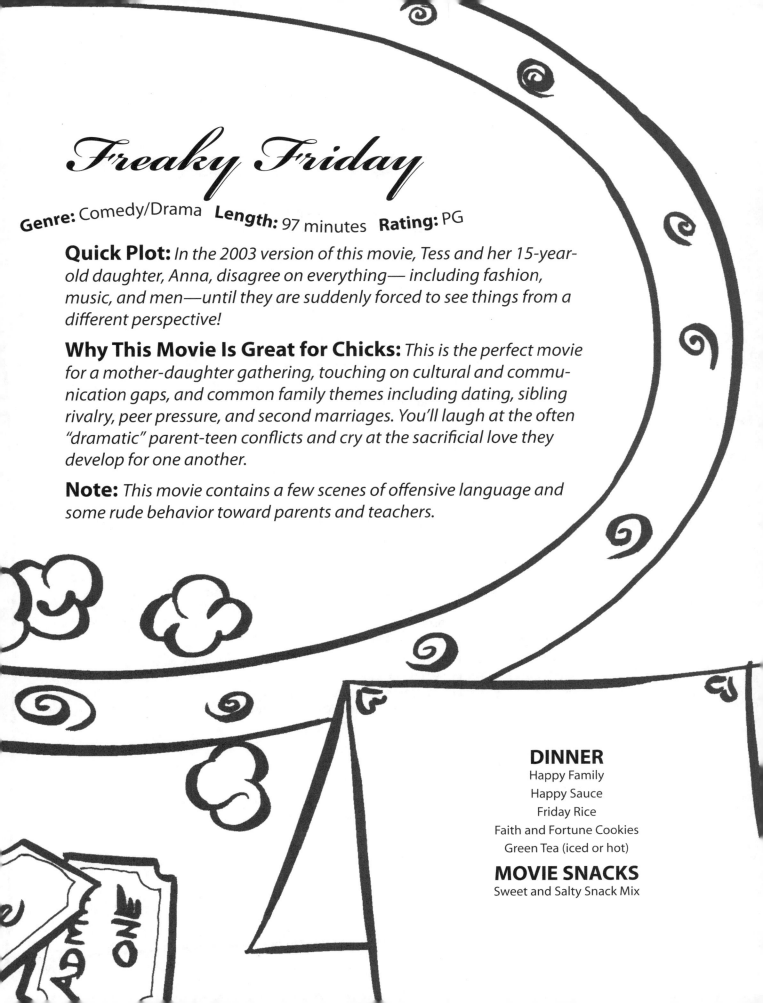

Freaky Friday

Genre: Comedy/Drama   **Length:** 97 minutes   **Rating:** PG

Quick Plot: *In the 2003 version of this movie, Tess and her 15-year-old daughter, Anna, disagree on everything— including fashion, music, and men—until they are suddenly forced to see things from a different perspective!*

Why This Movie Is Great for Chicks: *This is the perfect movie for a mother-daughter gathering, touching on cultural and communication gaps, and common family themes including dating, sibling rivalry, peer pressure, and second marriages. You'll laugh at the often "dramatic" parent-teen conflicts and cry at the sacrificial love they develop for one another.*

Note: *This movie contains a few scenes of offensive language and some rude behavior toward parents and teachers.*

DINNER

Happy Family

Happy Sauce

Friday Rice

Faith and Fortune Cookies

Green Tea (iced or hot)

MOVIE SNACKS

Sweet and Salty Snack Mix

⚬~ SUPPLIES ~⚬

If you're cooking your meal together, you may want to talk to everyone in your group and divide the ingredients list before your event. Keep in mind that some items cost more than others. Perhaps several people would like to share the cost of the more expensive items while others each bring a couple of items.

If you decide to have guests prepare the meal before the event, photocopy the recipes in this book and assign each recipe to one woman.

RECIPES

HAPPY FAMILY

4 large boneless chicken breasts, cut into chunks

2 each yellow and red bell peppers, cut into chunks

1 cup shredded carrots

2 cups broccoli florets

one 8-ounce can pineapple tidbits, drained

1 cup cashew pieces

1 cup flour

6 tablespoons olive oil

½ teaspoon each salt and pepper

Happy Sauce (see recipe on page 70)

This recipe is a fun and easy adaptation of the popular Chinese dish called Happy Family. Chicken, veggies, fruit, and nuts combine with a special sweet–and–sour sauce to make a yummy dish that will make a whole family happy!

Prepare the chicken and uncut vegetables by cutting them into stir-fry-sized pieces. Set an oversized frying pan or wok on high and add 3 tablespoons of oil. Place flour, salt, and pepper in zippered bag and toss chicken pieces in flour mixture to coat. Stir-fry chicken pieces in pan, stirring often, until golden brown and cooked through. Transfer to holding dish while preparing vegetables.

Add 3 more tablespoons of oil to pan and stir fry peppers, carrots, and broccoli until tender-crisp. Reduce heat and return chicken to pan just to reheat. Serve on individual plates and then ladle Happy Sauce over mixture. Sprinkle pineapple tidbits and cashews on top, and serve with a side of Friday Rice. Serves 8.

Easy Option Meal

Life too hectic to cook? Pick up a quick dinner to-go at your favorite Chinese restaurant. Order Happy Family or your favorite Chinese dish with sides of fried rice and fortune cookies. Pick up bottled green tea and a sweet and salty snack mix at your local supermarket.

RECIPES

FRIDAY RICE

2 cups water

2 cups instant white rice

2 teaspoons chicken bouillon

4 tablespoons soy sauce

2 teaspoons vegetable oil

½ cup chopped onion

2 eggs, beaten

½ cup peas (optional)

pepper to taste

This tasty fried rice recipe is a snap to cook. Place water, bouillon, and soy sauce in a pan and bring to a boil. Stir in rice, cover, and remove from heat. Let stand 5 minutes or until liquid is absorbed.

Heat oil in frying pan over medium heat, and sauté onions for about 3 minutes. Add beaten eggs and stir until eggs are cooked through. Mix in the cooked rice and peas and heat through. Season with pepper, and serve as a side dish for Happy Family. Serves 8.

FAITH AND FORTUNE COOKIES

3 egg whites

½ cup confectioners' sugar

½ cup flour

3 tablespoons melted butter

baking parchment paper

Making your own fortune cookies is actually easy and fun, and a great mother-daughter activity! You may want to ask someone to prepare these ahead to save time during your movie event, or set up two teams for efficient preparation and assembly before or after cooking your dinner recipes.

Prepare faith and fortune inserts for cookies using small strips of paper with favorite proverbs or Scripture passages on them. When these are done, preheat the oven to 375 degrees.

To prepare cookie dough, separate egg whites and beat with a mixer until just frothy. Add the confectioners' sugar and butter, and stir until batter is smooth. Stir in the flour and then let batter rest for 15 minutes.

While dough is resting, line a cookie sheet with baking parchment paper and draw four evenly spaced circles on the paper by tracing around a standard-sized coffee mug. Cut around each circle leaving about a half an inch extra outside edge. Repeat process to make about 12 reusable templates. Turn papers upside down so trace marks are against the baking sheet. Place muffin tin nearby to use in shaping cookies after baking.

Spread 1 teaspoon of batter on each paper round with a flat bladed knife, spreading thin to follow the shape of the traced circle. Bake in oven for 4 minutes or until edges begin to brown.

After removing cookies from the oven, work quickly and carefully—the cookies are hot! (Using cotton gloves when handling hot cookies is a good idea to prevent burns.) Lay one paper "fortune" in the middle of

(continued on next page)

RECIPES

each cookie, then hold cookie by the extra edge of paper and fold in half. Pick up cookie with paper and drape straight folded edge over edge of muffin cup to form cookie shape. Place cookie inside muffin cup to hold shape while cooling. Repeat process quickly with each remaining cookie. Carefully peel paper off cooled cookies and reuse. Repeat baking and shaping cookies 4 at a time until complete. Recipe makes approximately 24 cookies.

Note: For best results be sure dough is spread thin and fold dough as quickly as possible after removing from oven. Dough can also be colored with food coloring for special occasions.

SWEET AND SALTY SNACK MIX

1 large can mixed nuts

1 large can honey roasted nuts

1 bag sesame and/or pretzel sticks

1 bag yogurt-covered raisins

Mix ingredients together in a large bowl for a sweet and salty snack mix. Serves 8.

 Make Ahead of Time

HAPPY SAUCE

3 cups water

4 tablespoons orange juice

½ cup lemon juice

⅔ cup rice vinegar

5 tablespoons soy sauce

2 tablespoons grated orange zest

1 teaspoon minced fresh ginger root

1 teaspoon minced garlic

4 tablespoons chopped green onion

½ teaspoon red pepper flakes

2 cups packed brown sugar

6 tablespoons cornstarch

4 tablespoons water

This delicious stir-fry and dipping sauce is sure to become a family favorite and will motivate your guests to proclaim, "It tastes better than a restaurant!" For ease of cooking in the kitchen during your movie event, make this sauce ahead and gently reheat before serving over your Happy Family stir fry.

Pour 3 cups water, orange juice, lemon juice, rice vinegar, and soy sauce in large saucepan set on medium-high heat. Stir in the orange zest, ginger, garlic, chopped green onion, and red pepper flakes. Add brown sugar and stir gently until mixture comes to a boil. Mix cornstarch and 4 tablespoons water together and add to sauce. Reduce heat to low and stir until sauce is thickened. Ladle over stir fry and enjoy! Serves 8.

Decorations

This movie is perfect for a mother-teenage daughter event. To get into the switching-role theme of the movie, ask your guests to come dressed in an opposite role—either as a teenage daughter or as a mother. Keep the theme going by mixing up your décor with some decorations a teen would like and some a mom would like. Hang an inexpensive bead curtain across your entrance, and use a combination of modern colorful plates and vintage china to set your table. You might even choose to serve drinks to teens in goblets and the moms in plastic! Enlist a teen for advice on music, and play favorite tunes from each generation in the background during dinner. For some hilarious laughs, test your guests' talents with a karaoke contest before or after the movie!

COOKING TOGETHER

1. Assemble ingredients and supplies for cooking Happy Family stir fry and Friday Rice before your guests arrive, including pans, cutting boards, knives, measuring cups, and utensils. Place pre-made Happy Sauce in pan for reheating.

2. When your guests arrive, have small groups of two or three prepare the Happy Family stir fry and the Friday Rice according to the recipes. Have other guests prepare remaining foods, set the table, pour tea, and pitch in where needed.

3. If you're making Faith and Fortune Cookies after dinner, you could enlist a couple of extra volunteers to help prepare the "fortune" inserts and draw the paper parchment circles while the others are cooking.

4. When everything is ready, ask someone to pray, and then serve. Spoon Happy Family onto individual plates, ladle Happy Sauce on top, sprinkle with cashews and pineapple, and serve with a side of Friday Rice for a delicious meal!

5. When you've finished eating, clean up the dishes and put leftovers in the refrigerator.

6. Make Faith and Fortune cookies together according to the recipe, or enjoy pre-made cookies with hot green tea before or after the movie.

7. Place Sweet and Salty Snack Mix in a large bowl, and have small cups available for guests to serve themselves during the movie.

Helpful Hint

Be sure everyone washes her hands before the cooking begins.

Mealtime TalkStarters

- Share a funny story about experiencing a mother-daughter generation gap in your family.

- Our meal was called "Happy Family." How are the mixed ingredients in our dinner (fruit, meat, sweet, salty) like or unlike the ingredients it takes to make a real-life happy family?

LET'S WATCH A MOVIE!

Freaky Friday

THE PRE-SHOW

Bring the Sweet and Salty Snack Mix to munch on, and head to the area where you're showing the movie. Take this It Happened on a Friday Trivia Quiz and see how everyone does. Then it's movie time!

IT HAPPENED ON A FRIDAY TRIVIA QUIZ

1. What famous talk-show host was born on Friday, January 29, 1954?

2. What famous international sports competition began on Friday, January 25, 1924?

3. What epic movie premiered in Atlanta on Friday, December 15, 1939?

4. Friday was the last day of which two centuries since A.D. 1000?

5. What momentous event in U.S. history took place on Friday, May 5, 1961?

6. What "revolutionary" electronic device was released on Friday, June 29, 2007?

Answers

1. Oprah Winfrey, in Kosciusko, Mississippi.
2. The first Winter Olympics. The games took place in Chamonix, France.
3. *Gone With the Wind.* The governor of Georgia declared a state holiday for the premiere.
4. 1100 and 1900. Friday, December 31, 1999, was also the last day of the second millennium.
5. The first American, Alan Shepard, was launched into space. He spent 15 minutes above earth aboard the Freedom 7 spacecraft.
6. The Apple iPhone.

THE SHOW
Freaky Friday

Genre: Comedy/Drama

Length: 97 minutes

Rating: PG for some mild language and thematic elements

Plot: Tess and her 15-year-old daughter, Anna, disagree on everything, including fashion, music, and men. Anna is upset that her mother doesn't support her musical aspirations or school conflicts, and Tess, a widow, doesn't understand why Anna can't support her upcoming marriage.

One Thursday evening, their conflict boils over during dinner at a Chinese restaurant. Their fierce argument is suddenly interrupted by a Chinese woman bearing fortune cookies that, when opened, elicit a bizarre "earthquake." The next morning, Tess and Anna are astonished to wake up inside each other's bodies! If that wasn't peculiar enough, their Friday gets even freakier when they decide to switch roles for the day. The unique perspective they gain helps them develop a new trust and respect for each other, but with the wedding coming up the next day, they need to discover what it takes to switch back—and fast!

THE POST-SHOW

After the movie, use some or all of these questions to discuss the spiritual themes of *Freaky Friday.*

What was missing from Tess and Anna's relationship in the beginning of the movie?

Our snack mix combines both sweet and salty ingredients. How were Anna and Tess each salty? How were they each sweet? Which word do you think describes you best? Why?

How did changing places alter their perspectives of each other? How could changing places benefit us in understanding others in our own families?

Read this definition of love from 1 Corinthians 13:4-7:

"Love is patient and kind. Love is not jealous or boastful or proud or rude. It does not demand its own way. It is not irritable, and it keeps no record of being wronged. It does not rejoice about injustice but rejoices whenever the truth wins out. Love never gives up, never loses faith, is always hopeful, and endures through every circumstance."

Discuss whether Anna and Tess demonstrated this type of love to each other in the movie. How does this definition of love challenge you in your own life?

You may want to use these Bible passages during your movie discussion:

- 1 Corinthians 13:4-7—Definition of love.

- Joshua 24:15—Family commitment to God.

- John 3:16—God's sacrificial love for us.

- Romans 12:10—Honoring others.

What family conflicts portrayed in this movie are common to families today? Which are most common to you?

How do you think Tess could have disciplined Anna more effectively? How could Anna have responded differently to her mother?

Discuss how an act of sacrificial love changed Tess and Anna. How has Jesus' act of sacrificial love changed you? How has it changed your friendships with others?

PRAYER

Before heading home, make sure to end the evening with a prayer together! If you're hosting a mother-daughter get-together, you may want to take time to allow the moms and their daughters to exchange their Faith and Fortune Cookie Scriptures and pray a blessing over each other.

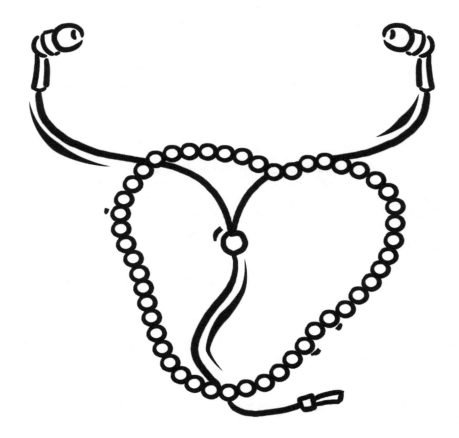

Cinderella

(Rodgers and Hammerstein version)

Genre: Musical **Length:** 88 minutes **Rating:** G

Quick Plot: *When a lonely girl is visited by her fairy godmother, dreams really can come true!*

Why This Movie Is Great for Chicks: *Didn't most of us wish to be princesses at one time in our lives? This 1997 version of Cinderella, starring Brandy Norwood and Whitney Houston, takes the long-loved fairy tale, adds music and humor, and turns it into an enchanting story with messages of encouragement for women of any age. This would be a great movie to show for a mother-daughter gathering, too!*

DINNER
Prince Charming's Cheesy Chive Chicken
Fairy Godmother's Fruit Salad
Princess (and the) Peas
Cream Puff Cake
Beverages (water, iced tea, coffee)

MOVIE SNACKS
Toasted pumpkin seeds (purchased from the store)

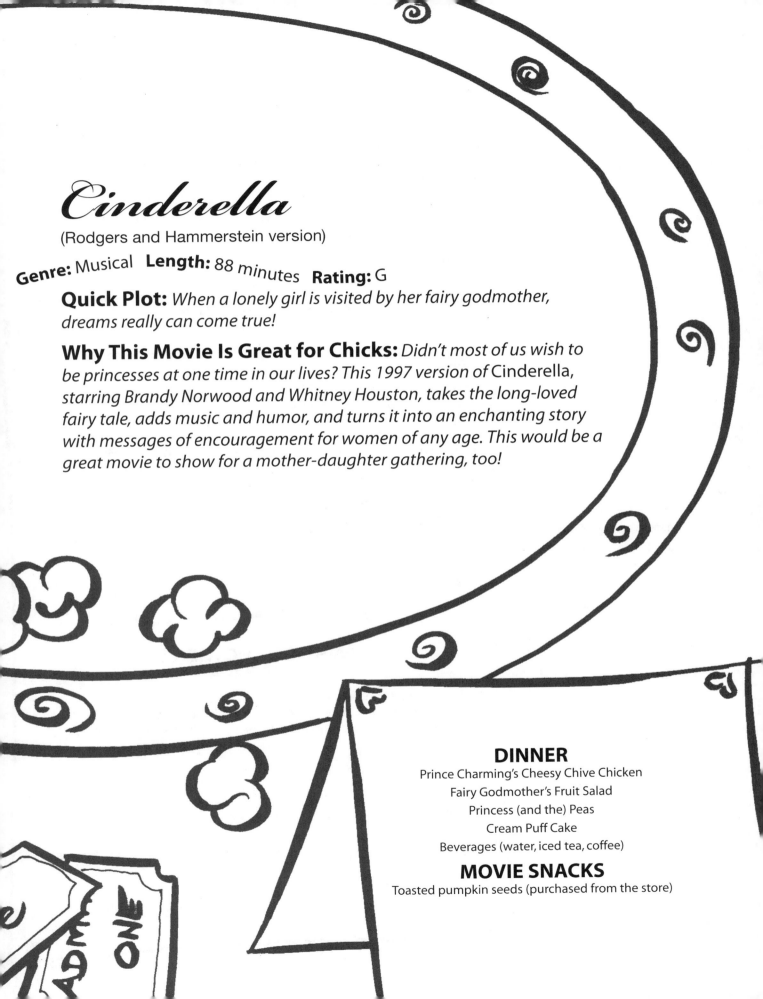

✷ SUPPLIES ✷

If you're cooking your meal together, you may want to talk to everyone in your group and divide the ingredients list before your event. Keep in mind that some items cost more than others. Perhaps several people would like to share the cost of the more expensive items while others each bring a couple of items.

If you decide to have guests prepare the meal before the event, photocopy the recipes in this book and assign each recipe to one woman.

RECIPES

PRINCE CHARMING'S CHEESY CHIVE CHICKEN

4 boneless, skinless chicken breasts

two 8-ounce containers of chive and onion flavored cream cheese

¼ cup Parmesan cheese

⅔ cup milk

1 package of fettuccini pasta

Cut chicken breasts into bite-sized chunks, and cook in a skillet until done. In a separate pan, mix the flavored cream cheese, milk, and Parmesan cheese. Add pepper to taste if you like. Stir over low heat until the cream cheese is completely melted. Mix with the cooked chicken.

Cook the pasta in boiling water according to the package instructions. Drain the pasta. Place a serving of pasta on each plate, and top with a generous scoop of the chicken sauce. Serves 8.

FAIRY GODMOTHER'S FRUIT SALAD

This is so sweet and creamy it's more of a dessert than a salad…but this is a fairy tale we're watching, so we can call it a "salad" if we want to! To cut back a little on calories and fat, use fat-free or sugar-free whipped topping.

1 can mandarin oranges, drained

1 can pineapple chunks, drained

1 small jar maraschino cherries, drained

1 cup of any kind of berries you like

1 container whipped topping

Mix all ingredients together, adding the whipped topping last. Serves 8.

Easy Option Meal

If you don't feel like being Cinderella yourself and spending time in the kitchen, pick up a couple of rotisserie chickens and a container of fruit salad (get the kind with whipped cream in it!) from the grocery deli section. Add a pumpkin pie from the bakery or a frozen one you can warm up ahead of time.

RECIPES

PRINCESS (AND THE) PEAS

Yes, we know that's a different fairy tale, but we just couldn't resist!

1 bag of frozen peas

Prepare according to the instructions on the package. Season with salt or butter as desired. Serves 8.

TOASTED PUMPKIN SEEDS

You can pick these up at the store already prepared, or if you can't find any, just serve other seeds such as sunflower seeds, or mixed nuts. After all, most of the characters in this movie are a bunch of funny nuts!

 Make Ahead of Time

CREAM PUFF CAKE

Lionel orders cream puffs for the guests at the ball to enjoy. This recipe is easy to make, and all your guests will feel like they're at the ball, too!

½ cup water

¼ cup margarine

½ cup flour

2 eggs

4 ounces cream cheese, softened

1½ cups cold milk

1 small box of vanilla instant pudding

1 container of whipped topping

small container of chocolate syrup

In a saucepan, boil the water and margarine until the margarine is melted. Remove from heat and add the flour. Stir until the mixture clings together and doesn't stick to the side of the pan. Add the eggs, one at a time, beating by hand until mixed in. Spread this batter into the bottom of a lightly greased 9x9-inch pan. Bake at 400 degrees for 20 minutes. Set aside to cool completely before the next step.

In a mixing bowl, beat the cream cheese and milk until smooth. Add the pudding mix and mix well. Pour this over the cooled puff layer. Refrigerate until the pudding is set.

Just before serving, spread whipped topping over the pudding layer. Drizzle with chocolate syrup, and serve. Serves 9 (so someone gets an extra piece!).

Decorations

Invite your guests to Prince Charming's ball! Suggest that everyone pull out those old prom dresses, bridesmaid dresses, or other frilly dresses that they never get to wear, and pretend they're princesses. Provide inexpensive tiaras (you can make them out of metallic chenille wires), and crown each guest as she arrives.

Twinkle lights add an enchanting touch when strung over doors or along railings. If they're in season, place pumpkins on your table or at the door. Some stores carry clear plastic "glass slippers," and these are cute on the table filled with candies.

For added fun, set all of your clocks so that they will strike 12 (or at least show 12 o'clock) around the time you anticipate the movie being over.

Helpful Hint

Be sure everyone washes her hands before the cooking begins.

Mealtime TalkStarters

- Who is your favorite princess (real or from a fairy tale) and why?

- Cinderella got her name because she sat by the fire all the time and the cinders smudged her face. What name would you be given based on what you do all the time? Perhaps Taxi-ella? Computer-ella? Shopper-ella?

COOKING TOGETHER

1. Have the first guest begin cooking the chicken, while another starts on the sauce. One of these guests can also get the water boiling for the pasta and cook that.

2. As more guests arrive, have them begin working on the salad and peas. Others can help set the table, pour beverages, and pitch in where needed.

3. Gather all of your ball guests to the dining hall, and thank God for your food and time together. Then serve the meal and let everyone enjoy it!

4. Once the main meal is done, have everyone clear away her plate, and then serve the dessert. Be sure to offer more beverages at this time as well. If you're serving coffee, now's the time to bring it out.

5. When you've finished eating, clean up the dishes and put leftovers in the refrigerator.

6. Get ready to watch the movie. If you're serving toasted pumpkin seeds as a snack, place those in bowls and make them available for nibbling during the movie, along with more to drink.

LET'S WATCH A MOVIE!

Cinderella
(Rodgers & Hammerstein's musical version)

THE PRE-SHOW

Serve the toasted pumpkin seeds, and head to the area where you're showing the movie. During your snack, take this Cinderella Trivia Quiz and see how everyone does. Then it's movie time!

We chose the 1997 Rodgers and Hammerstein version of Cinderella *for its beautiful music, great cast, silly humor, and its message of hope. You can adapt this party and the questions to use a different version of* Cinderella *if you like.*

CINDERELLA TRIVIA QUIZ

1. Who was the Frenchman who, in 1697, wrote the version of *Cinderella* we are most familiar with today?

2. In one of the earliest recorded versions of *Cinderella,* which came from China, what are the slippers made of?

3. There is an ancient fable that is similar to *Cinderella,* with the heroine wearing rose-red slippers. What is her name?

4. The Rodgers and Hammerstein version of *Cinderella* has been made into a television movie three times. Who played Cinderella in each of these movies?

5. How many princesses (real or fairy tale) can you name?

1. Charles Perrault
2. Gold
3. Rhodopis
4. Julie Andrews, Lesley Ann Warren, Brandy Norwood
5. Cinderella, Snow White, and Sleeping Beauty are a few fairy tale princesses; Princess Diana and Princess Grace of Monaco are a couple of real princesses.

THE SHOW
Cinderella
(Rodgers and Hammerstein version)

Genre: Musical

Length: 88 minutes

Rating: G

Plot: Cinderella lives with her insensitive and self-centered stepmother and stepsisters, who treat her as a servant. She longs to be loved and to have someone to love, but since she promised her father before his death that she would stay with her family, Cinderella doesn't see a way out of her unfortunate situation.

The prince, Christopher, is being pressured by his king and queen parents to marry. He wants to wait until he finds someone he loves instead of just picking a beautiful girl, but his parents are having a hard time waiting for him to find that girl.

The queen decides to throw a ball so Chris can meet all the eligible girls in the kingdom. Chris' objections are overridden, and the preparations are made. Cinderella's stepsisters eagerly attend the ball, hoping to be chosen by the prince, leaving Cinderella alone with her dreams. When she wishes to go to the ball, her fairy godmother appears, and we're guessing you know the rest of the story!

You may want to use these Bible passages during your movie discussion:

- 1 Corinthians 13—True love.

- Matthew 19:26—God makes all things possible.

- Esther—A woman who became a real queen.

THE POST-SHOW

After the movie, use some or all of these questions to discuss the spiritual themes of *Cinderella.*

Would you like to marry a prince? Why or why not?

What qualities are most important to look for in a prince (or in a husband) and why?

What wish would you want a fairy godmother to grant for you, and why? Is there any way you can make that wish come true yourself?

Cinderella has her own little corner and her own little chair as a place of refuge when she's feeling down. What's your special place of refuge?

Cinderella's step-mother says, "We hide our flaws until after the wedding." Is she speaking the truth or not? Share your thoughts on this.

One of the songs in this movie tells us that impossible things are happening every day simply because some people refuse to believe anything is impossible. What feels impossible to you right now? What could make that same situation turn into a possibility?

As the prince dances with Cinderella, he wonders, "Do I love you because you're beautiful, or are you beautiful because I love you?" Share your thoughts on this concept. Do we love others because they are beautiful…or do they appear beautiful to us because we love them? Could someone you know become more beautiful to you?

In the Bible, a girl named Esther becomes a queen, but her story isn't really a fairy tale. What similarities can you think of between Esther and Cinderella? What are the key differences? Which woman is more of an inspiration to you, and why?

What advice would you give to Cinderella's stepsisters?

PRAYER

Before heading home, make sure to end the evening with a prayer together!

The Philadelphia Story

Genre: Romantic Comedy   **Length:** 112 minutes   **Rating:** Not Rated

QUICK PLOT: *A woman and three men…whom will she choose?*

Why This Movie Is Great for Chicks: *This movie is every single woman's dream. Three eligible, handsome men all vying for your hand in marriage. While this can cause some interesting situations, it can also bring a few chuckles along the way, as well. Lighthearted fun coupled with themes of forgiveness, love, and truth equals a great movie.*

Note: *There are scenes of drinking and drunken behavior through portions of this movie.*

DINNER
Tracy's Cheesy Quiche
"Meat" Me at the Altar Quiche
Tootie-Fruity Salad
Refrigerator crescent rolls (purchased from the store)

MOVIE SNACKS
Triple Trouble Berry Bars
Sparkling cider (purchased from the store)

SUPPLIES

If you're cooking your meal together, you may want to talk to everyone in your group and divide the ingredients list before your event. Keep in mind that some items cost more than others. Perhaps several people would like to share the cost of the more expensive items while others each bring a couple of items.

If you decide to have guests prepare the meal before the event, photocopy the recipes in this book and assign each recipe to one woman.

RECIPES

TRACY'S CHEESY QUICHE

1 unbaked deep-dish pastry shell (9 inches)

4 cups sliced fresh mushrooms

½ cup diced onion

¼ cup diced sweet red pepper

1 tablespoon butter

1 cup shredded cheddar cheese

2 tablespoons all-purpose flour

1¼ cups milk

4 eggs, lightly beaten

1 to 2 teaspoons dried savory

1 teaspoon salt

½ teaspoon cayenne pepper

Line pastry shell with a double thickness of foil and bake at 450 for 8 minutes. Remove the foil and bake for an additional 5 minutes. Remove from the oven and cool on a wire rack. Reduce heat to 350.

In a large skillet, sauté the mushrooms, onion, and red pepper in the butter until the mushrooms are tender. Drain mixture and set aside. In a large bowl, combine cheese and flour. Stir in the milk, eggs, savory, salt, and cayenne, mixing until blended. Stir in the mushroom mixture, and pour into the crust.

Bake for 40-50 minutes or until a knife inserted in the center comes out clean. If needed, cover the crust edges with foil to prevent over-browning. Let cool for 10 minutes before cutting. Serves 8.

"MEAT" ME AT THE ALTAR QUICHE

The wedding is tomorrow, but who will Tracy meet at the altar?

1 unbaked pastry shell (9 inches)

½ pound ground beef

½ pound sliced fresh mushrooms

½ cup chopped onion

½ cup chopped green pepper

1 package (10 ounces) frozen chopped spinach, thawed and squeezed dry

1 package (4 ounces) crumbled feta cheese

6 eggs

¾ cup half-and-half

1 teaspoon pepper

½ teaspoon salt

Line the pastry shell with a double thickness of foil and bake at 450 for 8

(continued on next page)

Easy Option Meal

If you're short on time and don't have time to cook, stop at the grocery store and pick up a frozen quiche or two, along with a pre-made salad and a bottle of dressing. Indulge in the yummiest cookies or brownies you can find at the bakery counter—ones that will be sure to satisfy any sweet tooth!

RECIPES

minutes. Remove the foil and bake for an additional 5 minutes. Remove from the oven and cool on a wire rack. Reduce heat to 350.

In a large skillet, cook the ground beef, mushrooms, onions, and peppers until meat is no longer pink. Drain and spoon into the crust. Top with the spinach and feta cheese. In a bowl, whisk the eggs, half-and-half, pepper, and salt. Pour over the cheese.

Bake for 40-50 minutes or until a knife inserted in the center comes out clean. If needed, cover the crust edges with foil to prevent over-browning. Let cool for 10 minutes before cutting. Serves 8.

TOOTIE-FRUITY SALAD

2 cups fresh peach slices or canned peaches, drained

2 cups fresh blueberries

2 cups sliced fresh strawberries

2 cups seedless green grapes

1 package (8 ounces) cream cheese, softened

2 tablespoons lemon juice

1 teaspoon lemon zest

1 cup whipping cream

¼ cup powdered sugar

½ teaspoon vanilla

½ cup chopped walnuts

½ cup dried apricots, chopped (or another dried fruit)

In a large glass bowl, layer peaches, blueberries, strawberries, and grapes in the order given. In a bowl, mix the cream cheese, lemon juice, and zest. Set aside. In another bowl, whip the cream just until peaks form. Add the powdered sugar and vanilla, and whip until stiff peaks form. Fold the cream cheese mixture and whipped cream together and spread over the top of the fruit. Top with the walnuts and dried apricots. Serve immediately or cover and refrigerate. Serves 8.

TRIPLE TROUBLE BERRY BARS

These bars are in honor of the three men who pursue Tracy throughout *The Philadelphia Story,* causing trouble not only for her, but for her family, as well.

1½ cups sugar, divided

3 cups all-purpose flour

1 teaspoon baking powder

1 pinch salt

1 pinch ground cinnamon

1 pinch ground cardamom

½ cup shortening

½ cup butter or margarine, cold and cubed

1 egg

3 teaspoons cornstarch

4 cups mixed berries (raspberries, strawberries, blueberries, or other berries)

(continued on next page)

Decorations

Ah, the '40s. Invite your guests to wear knee-length skirts or dresses and a small hat (with a feather or two attached). And, if you really want to be daring like Katharine Hepburn, dress in a pantsuit!

To decorate, get boxes of all sizes, and wrap them in wedding-themed paper and ribbon. Set them on a "gift table" along with china, crystal, or glass goblets and candelabra. Place a couple of the smaller gift boxes and a candle or two on the dinner table as a centerpiece. On tables around the room, set out a few disposable cameras, and encourage women to take photos as they would for a tabloid event, snapping pictures when someone is least expecting it. Glamorous! If you have a digital camera, take a few pictures of the evening to print and give to your friends as they're leaving.

RECIPES

Grease a 9x13-inch pan. In a bowl, combine 1 cup of the sugar, the flour, baking powder, salt, cinnamon, and cardamom. Cut in the shortening and butter into the flour mixture, and then add the egg, mixing until dough is crumbly. Don't over-mix. Press half the dough into the prepared pan.

In another bowl, combine the remaining sugar, the cornstarch, and berries. Pour the berries over the dough, and then crumble the remaining dough over the top of the berries.

Bake at 375 for 45 minutes or until the top is slightly browned. Let cool before cutting into bars. Serves 8.

COOKING TOGETHER

Helpful Hint

Be sure everyone washes her hands before the cooking begins.

1. When your guests arrive, have the first few get started on the quiches right away, as they take time to bake. Since you will be making two separate quiches at the same time, it's a good idea to have one person in charge of each quiche. As others arrive they can join in with chopping, sautéing, and so on.

2. Once the quiches are well under way, have other guests make the Tootie-Fruity Salad according to the recipe. Cover, and place in the refrigerator until ready to serve. Other guests can help with setting the table and getting everyone something cold to drink.

Mealtime TalkStarters

- Do you read the tabloids or keep up on celebrity gossip? Why or why not?

- Is there someone in your life who has changed the way you see yourself?

3. About five minutes before the quiches are ready to come out of the oven, ask a volunteer to open the crescent roll tube and place rolls on a cookie sheet. When the quiches come out of the oven, adjust the oven temperature and cook the rolls following the directions on the package.

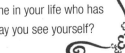

4. When everything is ready, place both quiches, rolls, and fruit salad on the table. Have everyone gather around the table, and ask someone to pray.

5. Enjoy the food! When you've finished eating, clean up the dishes and put leftovers in the refrigerator.

6. Serve the Triple Trouble Berry Bars and sparkling cider so guests can enjoy them during the movie.

LET'S WATCH A MOVIE!

The Philadelphia Story

THE PRE-SHOW

Serve the Triple Trouble Berry Bars with sparkling cider, and head to the area where you're showing the movie. During your snack, take this Katharine Hepburn Trivia Quiz and see how everyone does. Then it's movie time!

KATHARINE HEPBURN TRIVIA QUIZ

1. Katharine Hepburn holds the record for winning which award?

2. How many movies did Hepburn make with Cary Grant?

3. Was Katharine Hepburn married?

4. Hepburn was considered "box-office poison" prior to what movie?

5. What type of woman is Katharine Hepburn famous for playing?

Answers

1. Best Actress Oscars. She was nominated 12 times and won 4.

2. Four: *Sylvia Scarlett*; *Bringing Up Baby*, *Holiday*, and *The Philadelphia Story*.

3. Yes. She was married to Ludlow Ogden Smith in 1928 and divorced a few years later. Her most famous relationship was her long-standing affair with actor Spencer Tracy.

4. *The Philadelphia Story*, which was written specifically for her. Despite winning an Oscar in 1933 and being nominated for another in 1935, Hepburn had numerous films that did not do well at the box office. Additionally, she was known to be independent and headstrong, and wearing pantsuits and no makeup, which went against the culture of the day.

5. Strong and independent, much like herself.

THE SHOW
The Philadelphia Story

Genre: Romantic Comedy

Length: 112 minutes

Rating: Not rated

Plot: The day before Tracy Lord (Katharine Hepburn), a divorced socialite, is to get remarried, her ex-husband, C.K. Dexter Haven (Cary Grant), appears on her doorstep with reporter MacCaulay "Mike" Connor (James Stewart) and photographer Liz Imbrie (Ruth Hussey) from Spy magazine. Tracy is all set to kick them out when C.K. reveals that Spy has some dirt on her father. If she'll let Mike and Liz do an exclusive piece on the wedding, Spy magazine won't publish the story on her father.

Seeing herself thus blackmailed, Tracy lets them into the family home, and that evening they all attend a champagne-steeped party. In the wee hours of the morning, while under the influence, Tracy and Mike go for a swim. Upon returning to the house, they run into George (John Howard), Tracy's fiance. Assuming the worst, George calls off the wedding, leaving Tracy alone at the altar where she must make a decision that will change her life.

THE POST-SHOW

After the movie, use some or all of these questions to discuss the spiritual themes of *The Philadelphia Story.*

You may want to use these Bible passages during your movie discussion:

- 1 John 4:10—God loved us first, and gave Christ for us.

- Proverbs 15:23—The power of words and how they're used.

- Romans 12:17-21—Overcome evil with mercy and goodness.

Was there another alternative Tracy could have chosen when C.K. presented her with the story on her father? When have you felt trapped without a way out? What did you do?

Mike quotes a proverb that says, "With the rich and mighty, always a little patience." How does this relate to the storyline? What do you think of this proverb?

Tracy says, "I want to be loved…really loved." When have you felt this way? How could Jesus fill this deep longing?

Tracy felt deeply misunderstood. How did the words of C.K. and her father affect her confidence?

In what ways can you use words to build up or to tear down? Give a specific example of how positive words changed you. Who could you encourage with positive words within the next 24 hours?

Tracy and her father were able to find reconciliation and forgiveness. Would this have happened if her father had not spoken his heart? What is an example of reconciliation and forgiveness from your own life?

Do you think C.K.'s initial intention was to get revenge on Tracy, to win her back, or to protect her? How do you respond when you're unsure of someone's motives?

How did C.K., Tracy, and Mike each overcome evil with good? Is there a situation in your life where you need to let God and his mercy and goodness bring peace?

PRAYER

Before heading home, make sure to end the evening with a prayer together!

MENU

Dinner
Checkered
  Flagwiches
Tow Mater's Tractor
  Tippin' Taters
Lightning
  Lemonade
Race Car Cake

Movie Snacks
Kachow Dip and
  Chips
Flo's Soda

BONUS! Here's one extra movie for you from *Group's Dinner and a Movie: G-Rated*, which features friendship, faith, and fun for movie-lovers of all ages! We suggest you use this one as a mother-son event, or try it at home with your own family.

Cars

Genre: Family

Length: 116 minutes **Rating:** G

QUICK PLOT: A racecar living in the fast lane gets stranded in Radiator Springs—a quiet town from days gone by—and learns what's truly valuable in life.

SUPPLIES

Before your Dinner and a Movie event, you may want to talk to everyone who plans to attend and divide up the ingredients list. Keep in mind that some items may cost a lot more than others. Perhaps two people would like to share the cost of those ingredients, while others each bring a couple of items.

Easy Option Meal

For an easy racetrack meal, pick up a submarine sandwich for each person, or order one extra-long sub sandwich that'll feed everyone. Flo's Soda is a quick, easy drink (chocolate root beer floats), and Kachow Dip can be as simple as spicy salsa from a jar. Store-bought cookies and soda will complete the meal—so let the race begin!

CHECKERED FLAGWICHES

8 slices of wheat bread	¾ pound deli-sliced ham
8 slices of white bread	1 cucumber, sliced
8 ounces cream cheese	

Cut the crusts off the bread. Spread cream cheese on the bottom piece of bread, and then top with ham and cucumbers. Cover with a piece of bread of the opposite color. Cut each sandwich into 9 or 12 squares (depending on how big your slices of bread are). Rearrange the squares of the sandwiches by flipping over some of the squares so they resemble a checkered flag, alternating white and wheat. Serves 8.

TOW MATER'S TRACTOR TIPPIN' TATERS

1 package frozen tater tots or waffle fries	ketchup
½ of a 1.25-ounce chili seasoning packet	

Cook tater tots or fries according to package directions. Once cooked, sprinkle with the seasoning. Serve with ketchup. Serves 8.

LIGHTNING LEMONADE

½ cup sugar	½ cup lemon juice
¼ cup water	1 liter ginger ale
3 cups pineapple juice	

In a saucepan, heat the water over medium heat, and stir in the sugar, stirring until the sugar dissolves. Combine with the pineapple and lemon juice. Just before serving, slowly add ginger ale, and mix in a large pitcher. Makes 2 liters.

Recipes

KACHOW DIP AND CHIPS

2 pounds processed cheese (such as Velveeta), cut up

8 ounces cream cheese, cut up

one 4-ounce can green chiles

1 envelope taco seasoning mix

16 ounces chunky salsa

pita chips (enough for expected number of guests)

Combine the first five ingredients in a slow cooker and turn to low heat, stirring occasionally. Serve with chips. Serves 12.

FLO'S SODA

12 ounces (1 can) root beer per person

1-2 scoops chocolate ice cream per person

Serve these chocolate root beer floats for a fun movie drink. Simply place a scoop or two of chocolate ice cream in each glass and slowly pour root beer on top. Add a straw or a long spoon.

Make Ahead

RACE CAR CAKE

2 loaves of pound cake

2 tubs vanilla frosting

food coloring

4 chocolate sandwich cookies

black or red licorice strips

chocolate-coated candies

Remove cakes from pans. Cut 3 inches off of the end of one loaf (this piece will not be used). Diagonally cut 2 inches off of the top of one end of this loaf. Set this cake on top of the whole loaf, to look like a car. Spread vanilla frosting over the "windows" of the car—the front diagonal windshield, the back window, and the side windows. Use the licorice to line the edges of these windows. Add food coloring to the remaining frosting—whatever color car you'd like! Cover the rest of the car with the colored frosting.

Stick 4 chocolate sandwich cookies on the sides of the car for wheels. Use the chocolate-coated candies for head and tail lights. Use the licorice strips to create racing stripes and even create a number on the hood of the car. Serves 12.

TIP:

You can use any meat or toppings you'd like for creative Checkered Flagwiches—just don't make them too thick or they won't stay together.

ROUTE 66

Set the Stage

Decorate Nascar style! Create pennants with construction paper, and write the names of the cars from the movie on them. Hang black-and-white checkered flags on the walls—you can create them by weaving black and white construction paper together and attaching them to dowels. If kids are your decorators, they could have a lot of fun with both of these as craft projects.

Greet your guests with a homemade "Radiator Springs" highway sign on your front door, and label the dining area with a large banner that says "The Pit Stop." If you have any toy cars or classic car paraphernalia, such as posters, place these around your meeting area. If you have a DVD with footage from a car race, have this playing on your TV as guests arrive.

COOKING  TOGETHER

1. Before your guests arrive, assemble and frost the Race Car Cake according to directions on page 91.

2. Once guests arrive, remind them of the importance of washing their hands before preparing a meal.

3. Have an adult and a child team up to prepare Tow Mater's Tractor Tippin' Taters according to the recipe on page 90. You'll want to get these in the oven right away in order to serve with the meal.

4. Enlist an adult to help kids make the Checkered Flagwiches according to the recipe on page 90. Be sure the adult does all the cutting while kids spread the cream cheese and place sandwich ingredients on the bread. Have the kids arrange the squares into checkered patterns on serving plates.

5. Have an adult and a couple of kids team up to make Lightning Lemonade according to the recipe on page 90.

6. Have one or two more guests assemble the Kachow Dip according to the recipe on page 91. Be sure the slow cooker is set on low so the dip is ready for a movie snack after dinner.

7. Have any remaining guests set the table with dinnerware and beverages.

8. When dinner is ready, have someone say a prayer over the meal and dig in!

9. After dinner, ask a couple of guests to prepare Flo's Soda for movie snack-time according to the recipe on page 91.

10. Have the remaining guests pitch in to clear the table for a speedy cleanup!

LET'S WATCH A MOVIE!

CARS

THE PRE-SHOW

Have everyone gather in the area where you'll show the movie. If you've just finished eating dinner together, you may want to provide a quick break for people to use the restroom.

When everyone is together, serve Kachow Dip and Chips and Flo's Soda to anyone who's ready for a snack. Be sure to provide napkins.

Have adults team up with kids in groups of three to five, and give each group a piece of paper and pen. Ask groups to answer these trivia questions about transportation. Then read the answers aloud so all can compare their answers to the correct ones.

TRANSPORTATION TRIVIA QUIZ

1. How much does the world's most expensive car cost?

2. Which of the following has actually been clocked as the fastest piece of motorized furniture?

a. a motorized armchair boat

b. a wheeled sofa with a motor

c. a rocket-powered lawn chair

3. What is the fastest anyone has ever ridden a motorcycle—while blindfolded? (Don't try this!)

4. What year was Ford's Model T first available to purchase?

5. In which states does Route 66 begin and end? (For extra credit: What are all the states it goes through?)

Meal Time TalkStarters

• *Describe your absolute dream car. Why is it your favorite?*

• *Tell about a road trip you'll never forget. Was it fun? Did you get stranded somewhere? Who went with you?*

• *Have you ever visited a place that you didn't want to leave? Where was it?*

• *If you could win an award for any one thing, what would you want that award to be? Why?*

• *Which do you prefer, life in the fast lane or a Sunday drive down a quiet country road? Why?*

THE SHOW
Cars

Genre: Family

Length: 116 minutes

Rating: G

Plot: Rookie hotshot race car Lightning McQueen is at the top of his game—he's tied in a race with the top two race cars around, and he's on his way to the tiebreaker showdown. Being a celebrity, Lightning travels in style, cruising down Route 66 in the comfort of a custom trailer. But when he accidentally becomes separated from the trailer, he unintentionally tears up the asphalt of a forgotten little town called Radiator Springs.

The sheriff of the town catches Lightning in this act of destruction, and Lightning is sentenced to community service. But this hot rod doesn't have time for that—he's desperate to get back to his fast-paced life where he can prove himself on the racetrack and accumulate more trophies. He resents his punishment, and the slow-paced, simple life of the town's inhabitants just worsens his attitude. But after spending time with the cars of the town and making deep friendships, Lightning begins to realize that the things he's been chasing—awards, money, and fame—aren't the most important things in life.

THE POST-SHOW

After the movie, use some or all of these questions to discuss the spiritual themes in *Cars*.

 Which character in this movie reminds you of yourself? In what way?

 Which character would you most like to be friends with? Why?

 Lightning makes judgments about Mator and other rusty cars based on what they look like on the outside. Some of them also made judgments about Lightning. What did they learn once they got to know each other?

 Is it right or wrong to judge people from their appearances? Explain your answer.

Answers

1. $10 million—the asking price for a 1930 Bugatti Type 41 Royale Kellner Coach!
2. b. A motorized sofa in England has been clocked at 87 mph—and it's even licensed to travel on public roads!
3. 164.87 mph! A record set by Billy Baxter in 2003 in Wiltshire, England.
4. 1908.
5. It begins in Illinois and ends in California—going through Missouri, Kansas, Oklahoma, Texas, New Mexico, and Arizona on the way.

Lightning loves moving fast. Has anyone ever suggested you should slow down a little? What do you think about a suggestion like that?

 What does Lightning find in Radiator Springs that he hasn't found in other areas of his life? How does it make him feel?

 Getting praise from others made Lightning happy. Do you think he could be happy by praising others instead? Why or why not? In what ways can you praise or encourage the people you know?

 Lightning finds peace in Radiator Springs, but not everyone can live in a sleepy out-of-the-way town. How can you find peace where you are *right now?*

Bible Passages

You may want to use these Bible passages during your movie discussion:

- *Psalm 18:27—Be humble.*

- *Proverbs 27:2—Don't praise yourself.*

- *Matthew 7:2—Don't judge others.*

- *Mark 10:31—The last will be first.*

- *1 Timothy 6:6-8—Be content.*

PRAYER

End the evening by praying together. Ask for prayer requests. Encourage each person to share one specific way to live out a lesson learned from *Cars*. Have each person pray for someone else in the group; for example, everyone could pray for the person to the left.

Discover...

Group's Dinner and a Movie
Friendship, Faith, and Fun for Small Groups

Share a meal, catch a flick, and then talk about spiritual implications in the movie. Creates an electric, friendship-building atmosphere where you can comfortably talk about moral issues and biblical perspectives in today's culture. (Movies not included.)

ISBN 978-0-7644-2836-4